Enchanted Character Guide

Written by Beth Landis Hester and Catherine Saunders

Contents

Introduction

Step inside the magical tales of the princesses. This enchanting guide will take you through each story, from the very beginning to the happy ending. You will be introduced to every incredible character, and learn exciting facts about each of them, from their best friends to their biggest dreams. Discover how each one, whether good or bad, big or small, has an important part to play in every tale.

Hair black as night

Delicate collar

Skin white as snow

Snow White

Snow White was so
beautiful, inside and out,
that even the vainest queen could
not outshine her. When the young
princess was sent far away, she
found fun and friendship in the
most unexpected place.

Contents

The Evil Queen

The cruel Queen is cold-hearted, vain and obsessed with her beauty. She is so proud of the way she looks that she will destroy anyone who is more beautiful than her. She wants to make sure she is the fairest in the land.

Piercing green eyes

The Magic Mirror never lies. The Queen is the fairest of them all – but not for long.

High regal collar

Goal: To be the most beautiful woman in the kingdom – at least on the outside

Favourite colour: Inky black

Likes: Giving orders, magic, looking into her Magic Mirror

Dislikes: Pretty princesses

Once upon a time, a forest kingdom was ruled by an evil Queen. Every creature feared the terrifying Queen, who was also secretly a powerful witch. However, the Queen didn't care whether people liked her. She only cared about being the most beautiful woman in the land. Every day she asked her Magic Mirror the same question, "Who is the fairest one of all?" and every day the Mirror replied, "You are the fairest one of all." This made the Queen happy.

The Queen had a stepdaughter, Snow White, who was gentle, kind and good. She was also extremely beautiful, and the Queen worried that one day Snow White might become more beautiful than her. So the jealous Queen made Snow White wear rags and work as her servant. All day Snow White worked hard, sweeping and scrubbing. Snow White was happy in her work – she sang, daydreamed and had plenty of animal friends to talk to. Her greatest wish was for a charming prince to find her, so that they could fall in love.

Snow White

Snow White is kind-hearted and caring. Everyone likes her, especially the animals. Although her life is hard, Snow White is a hopeful person. She believes that good things will happen to her.

Patched, ragged clothes

Snow White loves making wishes at the Wishing Well.

Likes: Singing, daydreaming, helping others, telling stories

Dislikes: Messy cottages, bad manners, the dark forest

Belief: If you make a wish into a wishing well and you hear an echo, your wish will come true!

The Prince

The Prince is just as charming and handsome as Snow White dreamed he would be. He is perfect! The Prince is delighted that he has found his true love. He hopes they can be together forever.

The handsome Prince startles shy Snow White.

Bright red cape

Likes: Horse riding, singing to Snow White

Dislikes: Being apart from Snow White

Home: A grand castle

Dream: To find and marry his one true love

One day a handsome prince was passing by the royal castle and heard Snow White singing. He fell in love with her voice instantly. When he saw her, he fell in love with her beauty and grace, as well. Snow White was surprised to see the Prince. She was so ashamed of her ragged clothes that she ran away. However, when the Prince sang to her, she stopped worrying about her clothes and just listened to his beautiful voice. Quite soon, she had fallen in love with him, too.

The Prince decides to sing a beautiful love song for Snow White.

The Huntsman

The Huntsman has known Snow White since she was a little girl. He is very fond of her and doesn't want to hurt her. But he knows that the Queen will punish him if he doesn't obey her awful orders.

Unfortunately, the jealous Queen had seen Snow White's meeting with the Prince and she wasn't happy. Worse still, that morning her Magic Mirror had confirmed her biggest fear – Snow White was now the fairest in the land, not her. The Queen was furious and came up with a wicked plan to get rid of Snow White forever. She called for her trusted Huntsman and ordered him to take Snow White deep into the forest and kill her. She demanded that he return to tell her when Snow White was gone.

The terrible Queen wants proof that Snow White has really been destroyed.

Sharp hunting knife

Likes: Snow White

Dislikes: Being forced to carry out the Queen's wicked commands

Strengths: The Huntsman is usually loyal to the Queen. But this is not a usual order!

In the forest

Snow White loves nature, so being in the woods is usually a real treat. Animals have always been her best friends. She would never hurt another living creature.

Pretty bow

The Huntsman begs for forgiveness and tells Snow White to run far, far away.

Flowers, fresh from the forest

Cape to keep warm

The Huntsman watched as Snow White happily picked flowers and helped a poor little bird, who was lost in the forest. He realised then that he couldn't bear to do any harm to this kind-hearted girl. So he told Snow White about the Queen's evil plan and begged her to run away into the forest and hide.

The Huntsman returned to the castle and lied to the Queen, telling her that he had carried out her order. Fortunately the Queen believed what he said was true and she was happy once again.

Meanwhile, Snow White ran deep into the forest. It was dark and spooky, and soon she was lost and terrified. Trees looked like monsters and logs looked like alligators to poor Snow White. Eventually, she lay down in a clearing and wept. However, the next morning, the forest looked like a very different place. Snow White awoke to find herself surrounded by the sweetest woodland creatures. There were birds, deer, rabbits, chipmunks, racoons and squirrels and they all wanted to help her.

Forest animals

The forest animals are curious about the lost princess. They are a little frightened of her, too! But when they hear her sing, they know that she is someone very special. She isn't scary at all!

The forest animals are curious about Snow White.

Goofy, adoring smile

Home: Enchanted forest

Favourite food: Nuts, berries and leaves

Likes: Helping Snow White in any way they can

Dislikes: Being frightened

Seven Dwarfs

The Dwarfs march to work where they dig, dig, dig all day long. Their lives are rather quiet…and messy, until a beautiful princess comes along. They quickly realise that Snow White is someone special. They all adore her!

Doc

Sleepy

Bashful

Happy

The forest animals knew the perfect place for Snow White to hide. They led her to a tiny cottage where everything inside was small, too – even the furniture. Snow White felt sure that children must live there. She found names carved into seven little beds. Whoever lived there must be named Doc, Happy, Sneezy, Dopey, Grumpy, Bashful and Sleepy – and they were very messy indeed! Snow White set about cleaning, tidying and washing the cottage. Soon it was spotless and Snow White was so tired from all of her hard work that she fell asleep on one of the tiny beds.

Snow White decides to clean up the untidy, but adorable, little cottage.

A little while later, the owners of the cottage returned home. Doc, Happy, Sneezy, Dopey, Grumpy, Bashful and Sleepy were Seven Dwarfs! They were shocked to see that their home had been transformed and feared that some kind of monster had done it. They soon discovered that the "monster" was a beautiful princess. Snow White explained her problem and offered to cook and clean for the Dwarfs, if they hid her from the wicked Queen. The Dwarfs agreed, especially when she offered to make them gooseberry pie. Only Grumpy wasn't too keen – he thought that Snow White was trouble!

Grumpy

Dopey

Sneezy

Snow White and the Dwarfs sing and dance together.

Home: A cottage in the woods

Favourite food: Apple dumplings and gooseberry pie

Likes: Singing and dancing

Dislikes: Cleaning their cottage, washing before dinner

Evil old peddler

The Queen's magic potion changes her appearance and her voice. Snow White doesn't recognise her stepmother in disguise. However, her clever animal friends can sense that the old woman trying to sell her goods is evil!

Snow White was happy living with the Dwarfs and believed that she was safe. However, when the wicked Queen asked her Magic Mirror if she was the fairest of them all, it told her that Snow White was still the fairest!

The Queen was furious that she had been tricked! She looked in her spell books and made a potion to turn herself into an old peddler. She also created a poisoned red apple and, in disguise, the Queen set off to find Snow White.

Poisoned apple

Walking stick

Dark, flowing robes

The vile potion was made of horrible things, such as a shrill scream of fright.

The poisoned apple looks so juicy and tempting.

Snow White thinks the apple will make her wish come true.

Happily ever after

Snow White always believed that her prince would come one day, and she is right. The Prince breaks the evil spell and takes Snow White away to his magnificent castle. All her dreams have come true.

The Queen found Snow White alone. She gave her the red apple, and tricked her into eating it by promising that it would grant her wish. Snow White bit the apple, wished for her Prince and fell into a deep sleep! The Dwarfs were heartbroken and built her a glass coffin in the forest. One day, the Prince, who had been searching for Snow White, found the coffin. He kissed her and she awoke. Love's First Kiss was so powerful it broke the evil curse!

Pretty dress made of delicate fabric

The Prince's kiss brings Snow White back to life.

Flowing, yellow skirt

Cinderella

In a tiny kingdom, a young maid named Cinderella lived in a little attic room. Her days were long and full of hard work, but her dream of a better life kept her smiling. With hope in her heart and a little bit of magic, her wishes might just come true.

Contents

Cinderella

Cinderella is kind, gentle and ever hopeful. She never gives up believing that one day her dreams will come true. Perhaps someday she will even visit the royal palace!

As a young child, Cinderella lived with her doting father in a grand house in France. Their chateau was filled with love and every luxury. Little Cinderella had nearly everything a girl could wish for. Sadly, her mother had died long ago, and her father was upset to think of his beloved child growing up without a mother. So, he decided to marry again, choosing the elegant Lady Tremaine. She moved into the house with her two daughters and they became one big family.

Apron for housework

Cinderella's new stepfamily are always very well-dressed.

Home: A tiny attic room in a large chateau

Job: Servant to her mean stepmother and stepsisters

Likes: Having wonderful dreams, spending time with her animal friends

Cinderella juggles lots of chores.

Lady Tremaine

Lady Tremaine is graceful and well-mannered. She seems like the perfect lady. But underneath her calm appearance lies a cruel and jealous heart.

Expensive brooch

Cinderella's new stepfamily seemed nice at first. However, when Cinderella's father died, Lady Tremaine took charge of the household, and she became selfish and cruel. She forced Cinderella to work as a servant. From morning to night, Cinderella had to do all of the cleaning, cooking and sewing for her stepfamily. It was tiring work, but she still woke every morning with hope in her heart that her life would get better.

Likes: Money, ordering Cinderella around all day long

Dislikes: Cinderella being prettier than her own daughters

Goal: For her daughters to marry eligible men – grand dukes at the very least!

Drizella and Anastasia

Drizella loves to sing about nightingales, but her out-of-tune voice is anything but sweet! Anastasia dreams of being as elegant as her mother, but she is too clumsy! The two sisters never seem to stop bickering.

While Lady Tremaine treated Cinderella badly, her daughters, Drizella and Anastasia, were spoiled rotten. They were treated to fancy dresses, expensive jewels and a life of lazy luxury. They never lifted a finger to help around

As soon as Anastasia wakes up, she starts yelling out orders at Cinderella.

the house – unless it was to point and laugh at Cinderella. The vain girls were jealous of their stepsister's beauty. It made them feel better to tease Cinderella and give her as many chores to do as they could think of. The sisters were truly ugly inside and out. In their finest clothes, they could never match Cinderella's beauty.

Drizella's puff-sleeved dress

Anastasia's red hair

Likes: Sleeping in late, meeting rich men, having Cinderella wash and iron their many dresses

Dislikes: Finding mice in their rooms – they think that they are are horrible, ugly little creatures!

Talents: They don't have any!

Lucifer

Mean old Lucifer is a nasty cat, who is happiest when he is causing trouble! He chases the mice, teases the dog and messes up all of Cinderella's hard work whenever he can. This is one bad kitty!

Even the family cat, Lucifer, was treated better than Cinderella. He slept in a comfortable bed beside Lady Tremaine, and Cinderella had to serve his breakfast before her own every morning! Still, she always tried to see the good inside Lucifer, and the rest of the family, too. She believed that she should try to get along with everyone, no matter how hard it seemed. As the years passed, Cinderella grew into a very pretty young woman. But while her stepsisters paraded around at grand balls and parties, poor Cinderella never got the chance to go anywhere or meet anyone.

Wicked Lucifer is always thinking of ways to create problems for Cinderella.

Sly, nasty grin

Plump from drinking too much milk

Likes: Being pampered and spoiled, getting other people into trouble

Dislikes: Mice, baths, being woken up early

Favourite pastime: Chasing mice, bothering Bruno the dog

Mice and birds

The little mice are normally nervous around humans, but they know they can trust Cinderella to take good care of them. The sweet songbirds wake up Cinderella each morning with pretty whistles, and love to sing with her.

Cloth cap

Cinderella's only companions were the animals who lived around the house. She treated them like real friends, even making little shirts, hats and shawls to dress the mice and birds. She knew just how to make each animal feel special. In return, they did their best to take care of their "Cinderelly". They sang her cheery songs, mended her clothes and shoes and helped her in any way they could.

Scissors to help with sewing

The animals will always lend a helping hand.

Home: Various nooks and crannies around the house

Likes: Helping Cinderella – especially if it means tricking Lady Tremaine!

Dislikes: Being chased by mean cats

Cinderella loves Major and the old, faithful horse adores her, too.

Bruno and Major

Loyal hound Bruno often dreams about chasing and catching Lucifer! He doesn't mean to be unkind, but he can't help wanting to catch that annoying cat. His friend, Major, has known Cinderella for a long time. He is a very loyal horse.

Some of the animals, including Bruno the dog and Major the horse, had been Cinderella's friends since the days when her father was still alive. They were always ready to stop pesky Lucifer from trying to make a mess and create trouble for her. All of the animals were glad to see Cinderella when she came to the yard to feed the chickens, gather eggs and prepare breakfast for her stepfamily. When Cinderella was downhearted, they were always by her side.

Major

Bruno

Likes: Chasing and scaring Lucifer, making Cinderella smile and laugh

Dislikes: The way that Lady Tremaine and her daughters treat Cinderella

Favourite meal: Breakfast

The King

The King wants what he wants – and he doesn't want to wait! When things don't go his way, the King has been known to throw cups, chairs, weapons – pretty much anything within reach.

Meanwhile, at the royal palace, the King was planning a grand event. He was throwing a royal ball to bring all the maidens in the land to the palace, so the Prince could choose a bride. It was the King's greatest wish to see his son get married. He had always been a loving father, and now with his son grown, he was impatient to be a grandfather. There would be so many young women at the ball. Surely his son would fall in love with one of them!

Shiny golden buttons

Every maiden is invited to the ball, even Cinderella!

Dreams: His son getting married, having grandchildren

Likes: Romance, arranging grand balls

Dislikes: His son refusing to settle down, people making mistakes

The shining palace looks beautiful at night.

As the King's most trusted helper, the Grand Duke is a practical man. He is also a romantic at heart. After years of practice, he has become an expert at avoiding the king's tantrums, and the occasional thrown cup!

The Grand Duke was just the man to plan a royal ball. He was trusted with all of the most important jobs in the palace – including dealing with the King when he lost his temper. The Grand Duke tried to tell the King that the Prince would fall in love with someone and marry them soon enough. However, the King refused to listen – he didn't want to wait any longer. Afraid of upsetting him further, the Grand Duke started planning everything, and sent out the invitations at once. There would be a ball that very night – there was no time to waste!

Royal red sash

Likes: Doing his job well

Dislikes: The King's constant demands, having his ideas ignored

Greatest fear: Upsetting the King – the man has a terrible temper

Jaq

Daredevil mouse Jaq knows all the ins and outs of the chateau – including how to find the best snacks. He loves playing tricks on Lucifer, and creating diversions so that his friends can run away with snacks!

Sharp eyes easily spot food

The invitation from the king read, "By royal command, every eligible maiden is to attend." Cinderella knew that included her! Her stepsisters laughed at the idea, but she insisted that she had a right to attend. Her stepmother finally agreed that she could go – as long as she finished her work in time. Cinderella happily showed her animal friends an old dress that had once belonged to her mother. If she could fix it up, it would be perfect for the ball. But before she could even get started, she had to do her chores. Jaq knew that Cinderella wouldn't have enough time to make her dress.

Likes: Annoying Lucifer, cheering up Cinderella, looking for snacks, going on adventures around the house

Dislikes: Lady Tremaine and her daughters

Favourite food: Cheese

All the old dress needs is a few pretty ruffles and bows.

The mice escape with a roll of cloth for Cinderella.

Gus

Simple Gus gets very carried away by his love of a good snack. He doesn't always see danger! He's the mouse most likely to get caught in a trap – or by a cat's paw. But that doesn't stop him from helping Cinderella.

Shirt is too small

He came up with a plan. While Cinderella did her chores, the mice and the birds would surprise her by making her dress! Jaq and his friend Gus dashed around the house, searching for things that they could use. They took daring risks to grab an old sash and some beads that Anastasia and Drizella had thrown away. Not even Lucifer could stop them! Once they had everything they needed, the mice quickly got to work, measuring, cutting and sewing until they had created a beautiful dress for Cinderella to wear to the palace.

Likes: Playing with the other mice

Dislikes: Getting stuck in mouse traps, people screaming and yelling when they see him

Best friend: Jaq

Pretty in pink

Cinderella is happy that she is going to wear her mother's old dress to the royal ball. With some creative flair, her mouse friends have changed the old-fashioned dress into something young and modern.

Meanwhile, Cinderella had a very long day. Her stepfamily never stopped ordering her around. They knew that if they kept giving her extra chores, there was no way she would be ready in time for the ball. By the time the coach arrived, Cinderella hadn't even had time to wash up after her day's work, let alone make her dress. But when she arrived in her attic room, her animal friends had a surprise. There was her mother's old dress, but with new pretty sashes and bows – it looked simply perfect for the ball!

Old bead necklace

Handmade bow

Cinderella never dreamed she would have such a beautiful dress to wear.

The delighted girl put on the lovely dress and rushed down the stairs to join her stepfamily before the coach pulled away. But Lady Tremaine saw that Cinderella was wearing Anastasia and Drizella's old beads and sash, and she made sure that they noticed.

Cinderella's stepfamily can't believe that she is ready for the ball in time.

The spiteful stepsisters were furious and accused Cinderella of stealing their belongings – even though they hadn't wanted them anymore. They tore at the dress until they had ruined it completely. It was impossible for Cinderella to attend the ball now! Lady Tremaine and her daughters smugly walked out of the door, leaving poor Cinderella behind.

Torn to shreds

Even cheerful Cinderella cannot stay happy when her wicked stepsisters tear her lovely pink gown to shreds! She is sure that her dream of going to the ball is over for good.

Messy hair

Ripped seam

Fairy Godmother

Cinderella's Fairy Godmother can be forgetful, but she is filled with cheer and kindness. She is going to make sure that Cinderella goes to the ball. Her magic is amazing to see – while it lasts.

Big sleeves store magic wand

Cinderella was heartbroken. She ran out to the garden and cried. For the first time in her life, she feared that her dreams may never come true. Just when it seemed like all hope was lost, a Fairy Godmother appeared. She told Cinderella she would help her go to the ball after all! With a flick of her magic wand, the Fairy Godmother transformed a pumpkin into a grand carriage, Major into a coachman, Bruno into a footman and four of the mice into horses.

Likes: Helping people with her magic, conjuring up beautiful ballgowns and slippers

Dislikes: Losing her magic wand, forgetting her spells

Favourite spell: Bibbidi bobbidi boo!

Finally, the Fairy Godmother changed Cinderella's tattered dress into a beautiful ball gown and her ordinary shoes into delicate glass slippers. But she

When Cinderella sees her new dress, she can hardly believe her eyes.

warned Cinderella: at the stroke of midnight, the spell would break. To Cinderella this was more than enough time. Attending a royal ball at all was a dream come true.

Ready for the ball

Cinderella's shimmering ball gown makes her feel like a princess! But it is her sweet nature and open heart that will really make her stand out from the other elegant ladies at the royal ball.

Sparkling head band

Long, silk gloves

Dress made by magic

A pumpkin turns into a glittering carriage.

The Prince

The Prince doesn't think he will meet his true love at a boring ball. The whole thing seems like a waste of time. He feels like he is being pushed too hard into finding a wife before he is ready.

Ornamental shoulderpiece

At the ball, the Prince met many women, but he wasn't interested in any of them. However, when Cinderella walked into the room, he couldn't take his eyes off her. After a night of talking and dancing together, the pair were in love. Before Cinderella knew it, it was nearly midnight! She rushed to leave the palace before the spell was broken. The Prince ran after her, but all that was left was a single glass slipper. The King ordered that every maiden must try on the slipper and the one whom it fitted would marry the Prince.

Likes: Making his own decisions, dancing a romantic waltz, taking long walks through the castle grounds in the moonlight

Dislikes: Boring balls, meeting many maidens, his father trying to control him

Cinderella loses one of her glass slippers on the stairs. But she keeps the other one as a reminder of her amazing night.

When the slipper was brought to the chateau, Anastasia and Drizella eagerly tried it on. Neither one could make it fit. Lady Tremaine tripped the footman so that the glass slipper smashed on the floor, to

Cinderella's other glass slipper fits perfectly.

stop Cinderella from having her turn. But to Lady Tremaine's horror, Cinderella revealed that she had the second slipper, which proved that she was the mystery girl! The Prince had finally found his bride.

Royal bride

Cinderella never stopped believing that her life could be so much better. Now all her dreams have come true. She is finally free from her wicked stepfamily and has all the happiness she could wish for.

Diamond earrings

Elegant, long-sleeved gown

A royal wedding at last.

Gold crown

Pretty pink dress

Long, flowing skirt

Sleeping Beauty

A dark curse from an evil fairy changed the life of young Princess Aurora forever. The magic of some good fairies and the love of a handsome prince were her only chance of taking her rightful place in the kingdom once again.

Contents

King Stefan and the Queen

The patient and gentle royal couple rule their kingdom with kindness. But their greatest hope has always been to have a child. Their dream will soon come true.

Kind eyes

Neatly groomed beard

Home: A magnificent castle

Likes: Greeting guests coming to the castle, spending time with their old friend King Hubert

Dislikes: Anyone who causes trouble in their kingdom

For many years, King Stefan and the Queen longed for a child of their own. They feared that their wish may never be granted. When at last a princess was born, they were overjoyed! They decided to name her Aurora, which meant "dawn", because she brought so much sunshine into their lives. To celebrate the birth of the new princess, the king and queen had a grand reception. They invited guests from all over the kingdom, who were excited to see Princess Aurora for the first time. As the guests arrived to give gifts to the baby, the proud parents looked on with love. They had never been happier.

The kingdom gathers to celebrate with the new royal parents.

King Hubert and his son, Phillip, bring gifts for the baby princess.

King Hubert

Jolly King Hubert is very excited about the engagement between his son and the daughter of his best friend! He hopes that the marriage will one day bring the two kingdoms together.

Goblet held high in celebration

Tiny beard

In a nearby kingdom, King Hubert lived with his young son, Phillip. Hubert and Stefan were good friends, and for many years they had hoped to join their kingdoms together as one. A royal wedding would be the perfect way to do this – but it would be a long time before the royal children were old enough. For the time being, Hubert and Stefan celebrated the idea of their children living happily ever after.

Likes: Making toasts, coming up with great plans, getting his own way

Dislikes: His plans being ignored

Dreams: For Aurora to marry his son, Phillip

Flora

Kind but firm Flora is the leader of the good fairies. She is often the most sensible of the three fairies – although she can get pretty excited about the colour pink!

The fairies can't wait to meet the new princess.

Red, pointy hat

Likes: Granting amazing magical gifts, thinking of great ideas, bossing the other fairies around

Dislikes: People who use dark magic

Favourite colour: Pink

Among the well-wishers at the royal celebration were three good fairies, Flora, Fauna and Merryweather. The magical group flew gently into the grand hall, their kindly faces beaming with joy and love for the baby girl. They told King Stefan and the Queen that they would use their magic to grant three gifts to Aurora – one from each fairy. They decided to give truly thoughtful presents to the girl who would grow up with everything she could ever wish for. Flora, the leader of the fairies, was the first to offer something to the princess.

Flora gave Aurora the gift of beauty. She promised that the child would grow up to have hair as golden as the sunshine and rose-red lips. Fauna was the second fairy to give her gift to the baby girl. The kind and gentle fairy was enchanted by the little princess. She chose to give Aurora the gift of song, so that she would grow up to have the loveliest voice in the land. The princess would spend her days singing as sweetly as any nightingale.

Fauna gives little Aurora the gift of song and music.

Fauna

Sweet and loving Fauna always thinks the best of everyone. Like all good fairies, her magic can only be used for good – and that suits this gentle fairy just fine.

Magic wand

Likes: Romance, happy endings, baking – although she isn't very good at it!

Dislikes: Arguments, people who can't understand love

Favourite drink: A nice cup of tea

Maleficent

Maleficent is a truly evil fairy. She is very powerful, and can hold a grudge for many years. It is very easy to get on her bad side. The King and Queen made her angry by leaving her out of a party!

Black horns

Glowing green orb

Flowing, black cape

Home: The Forbidden Mountain

Likes: Power, evil plots, revenge, using dark magic

Dislikes: Stupid beings, not being invited to royal celebrations

Suddenly, an uninvited guest appeared in a flurry of bad magic. It was the wicked Maleficent – an evil fairy. She was furious that she hadn't been invited to the celebration. To get her revenge, she put a terrible curse on the young princess: by sunset on Aurora's sixteenth birthday, the princess would prick her finger on the spindle of a spinning wheel and die! King Stefan ordered his guards to seize Maleficent, but it was too late. After casting her spell, she vanished as suddenly as she had appeared.

Maleficent disappears in a burst of flames. Even the royal guards cannot stop her.

Maleficent's curse seemed unstoppable, but there was still a ray of hope. The third fairy, Merryweather, still had her gift to give the princess. She would never be able to undo such a powerful curse, but she had enough magic to change it a little with her own gift. Merryweather altered the curse so that if Aurora did prick her finger on a spinning wheel, she would fall into a deep, enchanted sleep. Only True Love's Kiss could wake her and break the spell.

Merryweather

Merryweather is not afraid to speak her mind and is fiercely loyal to the people (and fairies) she loves. When things don't go her way, this tricky fairy might just turn someone into a toad!

Delicate wings

The King and Queen feel helpless. Their precious baby is cursed!

Likes: Using magic, the thought of turning Maleficent into something slimy!

Dislikes: Flora bossing her around, not having her wand or wings

Favourite colour: Blue

Goons

Maleficent's henchmen are tough and eager to obey her. However, they're not smart enough to get the job done. They hunt for Aurora for years, but never find her.

Wicked expression

Yellow, beady eyes

King Stefan wanted to protect his daughter from the terrible curse, so he had every spinning wheel in the kingdom burned. But the fairies knew that wouldn't be enough to stop Maleficent. They came up with a plan to take Aurora away from the castle. Maleficent and her goons would be searching for a princess, so the fairies would raise her as a peasant girl. The fairies would have to put away their wands and live as ordinary humans in order to stay hidden until Aurora's sixteenth birthday.

The King and Queen must say goodbye to baby Aurora. It is the only way to keep her safe.

Job: Searching for Princess Aurora, guarding Maleficent's fort

Likes: Dancing around large fires, catching people

Dislikes: Maleficent's temper

Weakness: Stupidity

Maleficent searched for Aurora for sixteen long years. She ordered her goons to search everywhere – the towns, the mountains, and the forests. But they never came close to finding her. As the princess's birthday drew near, Maleficent was furious to learn that the foolish goons had failed.

Maleficent is worried – she has very little time left to find Aurora.

All this time, they had been looking for a baby. They hadn't realised that Aurora would have grown older by now! The evil fairy was becoming desperate, so she sent her loyal raven to fly out and search for any sign of a beautiful young maiden. The raven was determined not to fail his mistress.

The raven

Maleficent's raven is smart and very sneaky. He uses his sharp eyes and high-flying spy skills to help find Aurora. The raven is always by Maleficent's side, ready to do her bidding.

Large wings help fly over long distances

Goal: To help Maleficent find Princess Aurora

Likes: Spying on people and telling Maleficent everything he sees

Dislikes: The three good fairies and their magic

Briar Rose

Briar Rose is a simple peasant girl living in a cottage by the glen. She enjoys the simple pleasures of life, but in her heart she longs for something more. She doesn't know that she is actually a princess.

Briar Rose loves her aunts and their funny ways.

Golden hair

Simple, peasant dress

Home: A humble woodcutter's cottage in the forest

Likes: Singing, daydreaming, animals, long walks, picking berries

Dislikes: Being treated like a child, feeling lonely

Aurora grew up as an ordinary girl with a new name – Briar Rose. She lived with the three fairies, who she called her "aunts", and kept busy by taking walks through the forest. On Briar Rose's sixteenth birthday, the fairies hoped that by sunset, she would have escaped the curse. Soon she would be able to return to her life as a princess. They planned to give her a birthday surprise, and they sent her out so that they could prepare. They used their magic to make Briar Rose a beautiful dress to wear when she returned to the castle that night.

Briar Rose wandered through the forest, singing to herself. She soon came across the animals who lived there, who were her only friends. She told them all about a handsome stranger she had dreamed about. She knew that her aunts had forbidden her from speaking to strangers, but she wished they would stop treating her like a child. It was impossible to make any real friends! The animals tried to cheer her up by dancing with her.

Forest animals

The lively forest animals love nothing more than playing with the pretty and kind Briar Rose. They love thinking of ideas that will bring a smile to the face of their human friend.

Long, bushy tail

The animals love listening to Briar Rose sing.

Likes: Playing and being silly, singing, listening to Briar Rose's stories and dreams

Dislikes: Briar Rose being sad

Talent: Dancing with Briar Rose

Prince Phillip

Prince Phillip is brave, handsome and strong. He respects his father King Hubert, and does not wish to disobey him, but will not ignore what is in his heart! He is determined to marry the woman he loves.

Red cape

Nearby, Prince Phillip was riding his horse, Samson.

He was on his way to meet his intended bride, Aurora, at the royal castle when he heard Briar Rose singing. He was enchanted by her voice, and quickly followed it. When he found Briar Rose, he couldn't resist dancing with her. At first Briar Rose was startled by the handsome stranger, but he told her that they had met before – once upon a dream. Although she didn't know his name, as they danced, she found herself falling in love.

Briar Rose has finally found the man from her dreams.

Dream: To marry someone whom he loves

Likes: Beautiful music

Dislikes: Falling off his horse

Talent: Sword fighting – he can defeat any foe.

Briar Rose loves the beautiful dress and huge cake. This is a special birthday indeed!

Samson

Samson is one of the most impressive horses in the royal stables, and also Phillip's best friend. He is happy to go on adventurous rides, but he sometimes needs an extra carrot to go off the beaten path!

Sheepish grin

Strong legs for running

All too soon, Briar Rose had to return home, but she invited her new friend to the cottage that evening. She couldn't wait to tell her aunts that she was in love! When she arrived at the cottage, she was overjoyed to find a birthday surprise waiting for her. But this joy was not to last. When she told her aunts that she had met someone, they gently told her that she could never see him again. She was really a princess who was promised to marry Prince Phillip, and she must go to the castle that very night to meet him.

Favourite food: Carrots

Qualities: Loyal, strong and fearless

Likes: Riding with Prince Phillip. He's the fastest horse in the kingdom and can outrun anything that chases them!

Princess Aurora

Dutiful Aurora returns to the castle, though her heart lies elsewhere. She knows she could be happy if only she could see the handsome stranger again!

Maleficent's spell leads Aurora to a glowing spinning wheel.

Royal crown

Gold necklace

Stunning gown in Merryweather's favourite colour

Heartbroken Aurora did not want to leave her new friend behind, but she rode to the castle that night. What she and the fairies didn't know was that Maleficent's raven had discovered their secret. He had spotted puffs of magic coming from the cottage when the fairies had been preparing Aurora's dress. Maleficent knew where the princess was and followed her to the castle! As soon as Aurora was left alone, Maleficent used her evil magic to lure her to the fateful spinning wheel. Aurora pricked her finger and fell into an enchanted sleep. But not all hope was lost. The fairies realised that Phillip was the man Aurora had met in the forest. He was her true love!

When Phillip went to the cottage that night, Maleficent captured him, to keep him away from Aurora. But the fairies came looking for the prince and used their magic to set him free. As Phillip battled against Maleficent, the furious fairy turned herself into a dragon. With help

The fairies give Phillip the Sword of Truth and Shield of Virtue to fight Maleficent.

from the fairies, Phillip defeated her once and for all. He found the princess and broke the spell with a kiss. Aurora awoke to find that Prince Phillip was the man she had fallen in love with! Everyone in the castle was delighted to see their princess back where she belonged.

True Love's Kiss breaks the curse.

Maleficent the dragon

In a final fierce battle, Maleficent's evil powers take a frightening new form. She turns into a terrifying dragon! It takes all of Phillip's strength to defeat her.

Scaly wings

Breath of fire

Long, sharp claws

Seashell
earrings

Emerald-
green
dress

Shimmering
skirt

The Little Mermaid

In the kingdom of Atlantica, the merpeople lived happily in an underwater world. But curious Princess Ariel wanted more. She was willing to risk everything for the chance of true love and a life beyond the waves.

Contents

Ariel

Ariel has a beautiful singing voice, but she wishes that she could dance, like humans do. She imagines that the human world is so much more interesting and exciting than her underwater home of Atlantica.

Ariel lives in a beautiful underwater palace. But she wants to visit dry land.

Deep in the ocean lay the kingdom of Atlantica, home of the merpeople. A young mermaid princess named Ariel was bored with life underwater. She longed to explore the human world. Ariel often swam to the surface of the ocean to watch

Ariel treasures her secret collection of human objects

the humans on their sailing ships. She loved to collect human things that had fallen into the ocean, although she had no idea what they were really for!

Flowing, red hair

Home: A grand palace in Atlantica

Favourite Place: Her secret grotto

Likes: Singing, learning about humans, exploring shipwrecks

Ariel's father, King Triton, was the mighty ruler of Atlantica. He lived in a huge sea palace with his seven daughters. Triton loved all of his daughters, but he could not understand why his youngest daughter, Ariel, cared so much about the world of humans. What was so wrong with Atlantica? Besides, he believed that humans were frightful fish-eaters with no feelings. In fact, Triton had forbidden his merpeople from having any contact with humans!

King Triton

King Triton is a kind ruler and a loving father, but he hates being disobeyed. The entire ocean trembles when the king gets angry.

Golden trident

King Triton and Ariel love each other very much.

Job: Ruler of the Seven Seas

Likes: Listening to beautiful music, keeping his daughters safe

Dislikes: Humans, being disobeyed, arguing with Ariel

Weapons: A magical trident

Ariel's sisters

Ariel's six sisters are her best friends. They might fight sometimes, but these mermaid sisters always look out for each other. They think that the ocean is full of treasures…which make great hair accessories!

King Triton's daughters sing in perfect harmony.

Attina

Andrina

Ariel's six older sisters, Aquata, Andrina, Arista, Attina, Adella and Alana, were practically perfect princesses. They always did what their father told them to and never swam off on dangerous adventures by themselves, unlike their little sister. They loved living in Atlantica!

Aquata

The princesses were very fond of Ariel, but they did not really understand her interest in humans.

Adella

Ariel's sisters loved singing and had been practising for their next performance for weeks. They were due to sing at a party in honour of their father and they wanted it to be just perfect for him. Ariel was also supposed to be singing with her sisters for the first time, but she had missed most of the rehearsals. When the day of the party arrived, to her sisters' horror, Ariel missed the party, too! Where could the little mermaid be?

Arista

Alana

Ariel's sisters love her, but they find her very odd.

The princesses know how to make a grand entrance.

Likes: Singing, performing, spending time with their father, trying out new hairstyles and shell accessories

Dislikes: Ariel ruining things by being late. She never shows up on time for anything!

Flounder

Sometimes Flounder might seem like a "guppy", or a coward, but the little fish can be brave when he needs to be. He loves to help Ariel search for human things. He will do anything for his best friend.

Striped blue fin

While she should have been singing for her father, Ariel was actually busy exploring a mysterious shipwreck with her best friend, Flounder. The little fish was not a fast swimmer or as brave as Ariel, but somehow he always found himself caught up in her adventures. This time, the fearful fish was right to panic – he nearly ended up as shark food!

Shipwrecks hold many treasures, but they can be very creepy.

Exploring the ocean is dangerous. To this sharp-toothed shark, Ariel and Flounder look like a tasty snack!

Likes: Having fun, playing with Ariel

Dislikes: Spooky shipwrecks, being chased by scary sharks

Greatest wish: That he could be just a little bigger!

Ariel found some new "treasures" on the shipwreck, so she took them to Scuttle the seagull on the ocean's surface. She was sure that the nutty old sea bird would know what they were, and he did not let her down. Scuttle thought that he was an expert in human objects. He confidently told Ariel that the fork and pipe that she had found were a "dinglehopper" and a "snarfblat". Ariel was delighted, until she remembered that she was supposed to be somewhere else...

According to Scuttle, a pipe is a musical instrument!

Scuttle

Scuttle the seagull loves singing but sadly he does not have Ariel's wonderful voice. He thinks he knows a lot about the human world. Actually, his "knowledge" is a load of nonsense!

Webbed feet

Likes: Studying humans. He spends time trying to identify human objects, but he often mixes them up. He believes that a fork – or "dinglehopper" – is for brushing hair!

Sebastian

Horatio Thelonious Ignatius Crustaceous Sebastian, to give the crab his full name, has a talent for music…and for getting into trouble! He is also terrified of being eaten by humans!

Large claws for better grip of his baton

Down at the royal party, Sebastian, the court composer, was very angry. He was in charge of all the music at the royal concerts and Ariel had just ruined his most important performance! He was even more furious when Flounder revealed that Ariel had been on the surface of the ocean, instead of at the concert! Sebastian told King Triton that he needed to keep a close eye on his daughter. The king agreed and he asked Sebastian to spy on Ariel. It would be his job to check that she was not getting too close to the human world. Sebastian was not happy. He knew that a tiny crab would never be able to stop the headstrong princess from doing exactly what she wanted!

Sebastian is the most talented musician in all of Atlantica.

Job: Court composer

Likes: Writing amazing symphonies, conducting great orchestras

Dislikes: Upsetting King Triton, keeping secrets, getting into trouble

Grimsby

Grimsby is a majordomo, which means he takes care of a prince's needs. He thinks the prince should get married, but the prince will only marry for love.

Ariel can't resist getting a closer look at the fireworks on the ship.

Sure enough, Sebastian followed Ariel to the surface of the ocean. She was watching a firework display on board a nearby ship. She watched as a tall, thin old man gave a handsome young man a statue. While Ariel was spellbound by this amazing sight, lightning struck the ship and the young man fell into the ocean.

Fancy purple shirt

Grimsby gives a tall statue to the young man, who is actually a prince!

Job: Prince Eric's advisor

Goal: To help Eric settle down with a good wife

Dislikes: Listening to sailors tell ridiculous stories about merpeople – he is sure they don't exist

Prince Eric

Prince Eric is a kind, friendly prince who is happiest when he is sailing the ocean. He is looking for true love, and he is sure that he will know it when he sees it.

Ariel rescues the young man from drowning.

The man who fell into the water was Prince Eric – a human prince! He was unhurt, and he climbed back aboard the ship. Just then another explosion flung him back into the ocean. Ariel could not bear to watch him drown, so she rescued him. She took the unconscious prince to the shore, disobeying her father's orders not to go near humans.

Home: A castle by the sea

Likes: Sailing, playing the flute, dancing

Dislikes: Being told to find a wife – he wants to marry for love, not duty

Favourite place: His ship

Regal white jacket

Ariel has never seen a human so close before.

Prince Eric was so handsome that Ariel could not help singing to him. He was just the kind of human she could fall in love with. As the prince woke up, Ariel hurried back into the ocean before he could see her clearly.

When Prince Eric opens his eyes he sees a most beautiful face.

However, Prince Eric had heard her beautiful voice, and begun to fall in love with her. He had no idea that the voice belonged to a mermaid, but his clever dog knew the truth. Max had seen everything and understood exactly who Ariel was. Max was Prince Eric's best friend and most loyal companion. He liked the brave little mermaid with the wonderful voice, and hoped that Eric would meet her again.

Max

Max may not be able to talk, but he is very clever. The sheepdog has fluffy hair, blue eyes and a great sense of smell. He can tell if a person is good or bad, just by sniffing them.

Fluffy fur covers eyes

Best friend: Prince Eric

Likes: Playing fetch with Eric, being silly, meeting new people, licking faces

Favourite place: The beach near the castle – he loves taking long walks there with Eric.

Ursula

Ursula smiles and pretends to help people, but she only cares about helping herself. She is so wicked that King Triton banished her from Atlantica forever.

Ursula tries to use Ariel as part of her own wicked plans.

Creepy black tentacles

Powers: Creating magic potions, changing appearances

Dream: To take revenge on King Triton and rule the ocean

Likes: Power, making deals, ruining merfolk's lives

Unfortunately someone else had been keeping a wicked eye on Ariel's adventures – Ursula the sea witch. She was so evil, King Triton had forced her to leave Atlantica. Now she hoped she had found the perfect way to get revenge on her enemy, the king. She was sure that lovestruck Ariel would do anything to be with her prince. Even if it meant disobeying her father's wishes.

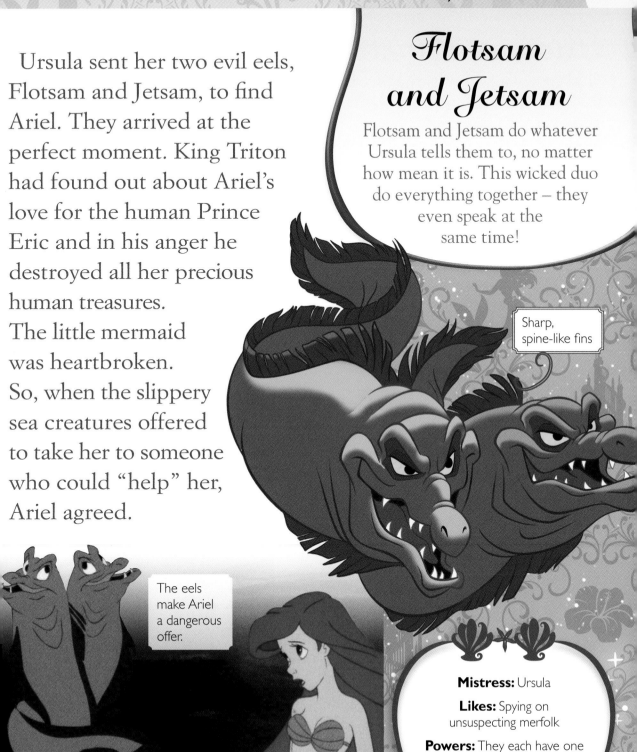

Ursula sent her two evil eels, Flotsam and Jetsam, to find Ariel. They arrived at the perfect moment. King Triton had found out about Ariel's love for the human Prince Eric and in his anger he destroyed all her precious human treasures. The little mermaid was heartbroken. So, when the slippery sea creatures offered to take her to someone who could "help" her, Ariel agreed.

Flotsam and Jetsam

Flotsam and Jetsam do whatever Ursula tells them to, no matter how mean it is. This wicked duo do everything together – they even speak at the same time!

Sharp, spine-like fins

The eels make Ariel a dangerous offer.

Mistress: Ursula

Likes: Spying on unsuspecting merfolk

Powers: They each have one magic eye, which they can combine to form a crystal ball. This lets Ursula spy on Ariel!

Human at last

Ariel has dreamed of having legs and feet like a human, but they are harder to use than she thought they would be. Finding human clothes is also tricky – she has to make do with an old sail and some rope!

Ursula offered to make Ariel human if she gave the sea witch her voice in return. However, there were conditions attached: if Prince Eric did not give Ariel a True Love's Kiss within three days, she would not only become a mermaid again, but she would also belong to Ursula. Ariel was so deeply in love that she agreed. Ursula took Ariel's voice and put it inside a necklace, and the happy princess set off to find Prince Eric, using her brand new legs and feet.

Sail cloth for a dress

Rope used as a belt

Real human legs

When Ariel agrees to Ursula's deal, she must sign a binding contract.

It is impossible for Ariel to tell Prince Eric who she is, no matter how hard she tries!

Carlotta

Prince Eric's housekeeper, Carlotta, keeps the castle running smoothly. She is a kind lady who treats Ariel like a daughter and makes her feel at home.

Scuttle helped Ariel make a dress from an old sail. She didn't have to wait long before Max's sense of smell led Prince Eric straight to her. The prince thought that she looked familiar, but when he realised that Ariel had no voice, he thought she couldn't be the woman who had sung to him. He kindly offered to help her anyway and took Ariel back to his castle. Carlotta, his housekeeper, would know what to do. Sebastian followed Ariel, but instead of helping her, he ended up in the laundry!

Housekeeper's simple uniform

Ariel feels at home back in the water again.

Job: Prince Eric's long-time housekeeper

Likes: Looking after people, keeping Prince Eric happy

Dislikes: A messy castle, dirty clothes

Chef Louis

Moody head chef Louis is a fantastic cook. However, he is as famous for his hot temper as his delicious food. Nothing makes him angrier than when things don't go his way in the kitchen!

Ariel may have changed, but she is still just as beautiful.

Floppy chef's cap

Likes: Singing and dancing around the kitchen, cooking delicious seafood for Prince Eric's court

Dislikes: Pesky crabs running away when he is trying to cook them!

Ariel loved life at the castle. Carlotta found her some human clothes and Ariel chose a beautiful pink gown to wear. Everything felt very strange and new. However, Ariel also found out that, thanks to Scuttle's advice, her table manners were a little unusual. She tried to comb her hair with a fork, or "dinglehopper", from the dining table! But at least her funny habits seemed to make the prince smile.

Things were not going quite so well for Sebastian though. Chef Louis tried to serve him up for dinner!

Ariel needs a good night's rest after her long day.

A real lady

At first, Ariel feels a little shy in the castle. However, she soon relaxes and her charming but odd habits make Prince Eric laugh.

A real human dress

Pearl earrings

Stylish colours

That night, Ariel had the best night's sleep of her life. She was sleeping in a comfortable bed for the first time ever, and she was also happy to be close to the man she loved. He might not love her back yet, but she hoped that he soon would. Back home in Atlantica, King Triton had no idea where his daughter was. He was desperate to find her and bring her home.

King Triton will not rest until he knows that Ariel is safe.

Adventurous Ariel

Ariel loves being human. She is curious to see everything and brave enough to try anything – even driving a carriage. If only she could sing about it!

Ariel finally gets to do something she always dreamed of – dancing!

Windswept hair

Sea-blue skirt

Comfortable shoes for exploring

The next day, Eric showed Ariel his entire kingdom. She was amazed by everything she saw – it was even better than she dreamed it would be. The young couple had fun and began to grow closer. Prince Eric even guessed Ariel's name at last,

Ariel and Eric share a special moment on a rowboat, thanks to Ariel's pals.

with a little hint from Sebastian. Finally, Ariel and the prince were about to share a kiss. However, Flotsam and Jetsam had been watching Ariel and they knew they needed to ruin the romantic moment.

Under orders from Ursula, the pair of eels tipped over Ariel and Prince Eric's boat. Ursula was very angry that Ariel had almost made Eric fall in love with her – even without her beautiful voice! The evil sea witch decided to take matters into her own tentacles. She disguised herself as a beautiful woman named Vanessa, and she wore the magical necklace that gave her Ariel's amazing voice. She planned to use it to hypnotise Prince Eric into believing that she was the singing girl who had saved him.

Vanessa

Vanessa seems to be a lovely young woman with a beautiful voice, but she is really Ursula in disguise. No amount of magic can stop Ursula's horrible personality from showing through!

Bewitching blue eyes

Long, dark hair

Magic necklace

Ursula's reflection shows her true form.

Finding home

Ariel now knows that she could never be happy as a mermaid. Although she would miss her family and friends, the human world is where she truly belongs.

Scuttle is determined to stop the wedding.

Beautiful singing voice

Sparkly purple dress

Ursula's disguise worked. Prince Eric was fooled by the sound of Ariel's voice and he asked Vanessa to marry him. Luckily, Scuttle realised the truth. He gathered a host of sea creatures to cause chaos at the wedding. They managed to smash Ursula's necklace, releasing Ariel's voice. Finally, Ariel had her voice back and Eric knew that she was his true love. However, it was too late – three days had already passed. Ariel had to pay the price for her bargain with Ursula.

Now Ariel was a mermaid again and she belonged to the sea witch. However, King Triton offered to take his daughter's place, and Ursula agreed. This had been her plan all along! Prince

King Triton is prepared to give up his throne to keep Ariel safe.

Eric was not about to give up on Ariel though, and he defeated Ursula. At last, King Triton could see that Ariel and Eric truly loved each other. He used his trident to make Ariel human again, this time forever.

Ariel and Prince Eric marry onboard his ship.

Royal bride

Ariel feels truly happy on her wedding day, with all her family and friends around her. She cannot wait to share her next adventures with Prince Eric.

Puffed sleeves

Glittering crown

White satin layer

72

Beautiful
rose

Off-shoulder
sleeves

Gold
embroidery

72

72

Beauty and the Beast

Young Belle lived in an ordinary town, where she could only find excitement by reading fairy tales. But a journey to an enchanted castle and a meeting with a cursed prince were about to make her dreams of adventure come to life.

Contents

The Prince

The young Prince has everything anyone could wish for, but he is selfish and cruel. He definitely does not want to help anyone in need – especially a poor beggar woman.

Crown studded with jewels

In a towering castle, a selfish prince lived a life of luxury. He never worried about what other people might need. He only thought about his own happiness and comfort. One night, a beggar woman arrived at the castle door, looking tattered and tired. She offered to give him a beautiful rose if he let her take shelter in his castle. But the mean Prince sent her back into the cold because he did not want to look at her ugliness. If only he knew how his cruelty would be punished!

Home: A shining castle

Likes: Servants who obey his every wish, people who are beautiful – at least on the outside!

Dislikes: People who are poorer than him, ugliness

When the Prince tried to send the beggar woman away, her ugly appearance magically transformed. She was now a beautiful enchantress! As a punishment for the Prince's unkind behaviour, she cast a spell over the whole castle. The handsome Prince became an ugly beast, and his servants changed into household objects. The only way to break the spell was for the Prince to learn to love – and to be loved in return – by the time the last petal fell from the magical rose on his 21st birthday.

The Prince is cursed.

The enchantress

The beautiful enchantress can disguise herself in lots of different forms. She uses a magic spell to teach the Prince an important lesson about kindness.

Curly, golden hair

Likes: Those who can see beauty on the inside

Dislikes: Mean and selfish people

Abilities: Casting powerful curses and transforming people into objects or animals

Belle

Belle loves to read books about romance and adventure. But in her town, nothing exciting really happens. Belle longs for a real-life fairy tale that will take her out of an ordinary life and into one filled with adventure.

Belle feels different than the villagers.

Practical white apron

Home: A small town in France

Likes: Reading, dreaming

Dislikes: Arrogance, people who have no imagination

Dream: To leave her town and have exciting adventures

In young Belle's tiny, quiet town, most people spent their days hunting, gossiping and swooning over Gaston, the most handsome man in town. Belle was different. She preferred to spend her time daydreaming and reading every book she could find. Belle was always friendly and polite, but to her neighbours she still seemed odd. Strangest of all, they thought, was the fact that Belle wouldn't agree to marry Gaston!

Belle's favourite kind of story often includes a prince in disguise.

Gaston's good looks and amazing strength were famous in the town. He just loved to show off for his adoring fans! No one could match Gaston's skill with a bow and arrow, or make the ladies fall in love quite as quickly as he did. All it took was a wink of his dazzling blue eyes. It seemed that Belle was the only girl in the village who wanted nothing to do with him. Unfortunately for Belle, Gaston was planning to marry her, and he would not take no for an answer!

Gaston

Gaston is handsome and he knows it! He is used to everyone noticing him. But in case anyone does not catch on, he will be the first to explain just how wonderful he is!

Quiver holds arrows

Dream: To marry Belle – since she is as good-looking as he is.

Likes: Looking at himself, talking about himself, hunting, showing off

Dislikes: Not getting his own way, looking like a fool

Gaston is sure that Belle will be his wife.

Lefou

Gaston's best friend is always by his side. Lefou would do anything for his friend. He cheers Gaston on and often helps him with his crafty plots. All Lefou wants in return is to spend time with his hero, Gaston.

Gaston's best friend Lefou thought that Gaston was just the greatest. However, even Lefou knew that his friend was not the smartest guy in town. After all, it was clear to Lefou that Belle was not the right bride for his buddy – but he knew that disagreeing with Gaston would earn him a punch in the face! Lefou decided that if Gaston was determined to have Belle as his wife, he would do everything he could to help Gaston get what he wanted.

Black bow tie

Lefou agrees with everything Gaston says.

Dream: To be as handsome and popular as Gaston

Likes: Hunting, plotting with Gaston, joking around, making fun of people

Favourite place: The tavern

The Bimbettes always like to be near Gaston.

Bimbettes

The three blonde, boy-crazy Bimbettes can't understand why any girl would turn down Gaston. After all, he is handsome and strong – and in their opinion, that is all a man needs to be!

Adoring looks meant only for Gaston

When Gaston's wedding day came around, he had not even asked Belle to marry him yet! He was sure that she would say yes, and that they would go on to have six or seven children together. Belle knew she could never marry a vain and stupid man like Gaston – even if the town Bimbettes thought she was crazy. Watching gorgeous Gaston strut through the streets was the best part of their day. But that was not the case for Belle! Gaston was not used to being turned down and he did not take Belle's refusal well.

Likes: Swooning over Gaston's strength and his good looks

Dislikes: Gaston paying attention to Belle

Dream: To win Gaston's heart, or at least get his attention!

Maurice

Inventor Maurice has a talent for building things and is obsessed with creating a brilliant new invention. But he cares about his daughter, Belle, more than any machine.

Not all of Maurice's crazy inventions work. But Belle is always by his side to give him support.

Tools for building gadgets

Likes: Coming up with crazy new machines

Dislikes: His inventions not working, being apart from Belle

Dream: To become a world-famous inventor

Day after day, Belle's father, Maurice, stayed tucked away in his workshop tinkering with his latest machine. Puffs of smoke and loud clashes and bangs showed that he was hard at work, even though most of his inventions never actually turned out the way he wanted. All of the neighbours thought that he was crazy. But Belle had total faith in her father and was sure that he would come up with something amazing soon. With Belle to boost his spirits, Maurice stuck with his work, dreaming that one day an invention would bring him fame and fortune.

When Maurice finally got a wood-cutting invention to work, he quickly set off for the inventors' fair with his trusty horse, Phillipe. He was sure that it would win first prize! But he soon got lost in the shadowy woods and was chased by screeching bats and howling wolves. Phillipe got scared and ran off, leaving Maurice behind. When Phillipe raced back home alone, Belle realised that something bad must have happened to her father. She and Phillipe quickly rode off in search of him.

Phillipe and Belle have no time to lose!

Phillipe

Loyal Phillipe is huge and strong, but not always the bravest of horses. He usually tries to make his journeys as easy as possible, and he always prefers the road home.

Leather harness

Likes: Giving rides to Maurice and Belle

Dislikes: Scary forests, flying bats, being chased by wolves

Greatest wish: That Maurice had a better sense of direction

Lumière

Charming Lumière cannot resist helping anyone in need! He is very happy to welcome people into the castle and offer them shelter, food and fun. Lumière is a true romantic and believes that the Beast can learn to love.

The Beast never lets strangers into the castle. Maurice is not welcome!

Hands are lit candles

Dream: For the Beast to find true love, so that he and the other servants can be human again.

Likes: Romance, putting on dinner and a show

Dislikes: Rudeness

Maurice ran through the woods until he came across the Beast's castle. He went inside to look for help, and there he found household objects that were alive and could even talk. A friendly candelabra named Lumière was happy to have a guest. But a clock named Cogsworth was afraid of what would happen when the Beast found out that a stranger was in his castle. Just as Maurice was getting used to this strange place, he came face-to-face with the Beast! Thinking Maurice had only come to stare at his ugly looks, the angry Beast locked him away in the castle's tower.

It was not long before Belle arrived at the castle. Lumière and Cogsworth were excited when they saw her – perhaps she would be the one to break the spell! Belle began searching for her father, and soon found

Lumière can't believe that there is a girl in the castle!

that the Beast was keeping him prisoner. In order to free her father, Belle bravely offered to take his place. She promised to live in the castle forever, which meant giving up her dreams of adventure.

Poor Belle has lost both her father and her dreams, all in one night.

Cogsworth

Stuffy Cogsworth is the head of the household. He takes his job very seriously! He likes things to run smoothly and doesn't like to break the rules. The last thing he wants is to get into trouble with the Beast!

Swinging pendulum

Goal: To keep the castle in order

Likes: Giving tours of the castle, following the rules, bossing the servants around

Dislikes: Being ignored, getting into trouble

Mrs Potts

As the castle's housekeeper, Mrs Potts always has plenty of work to do. However, she takes the time to look after everyone in the castle, and she always knows how to cheer someone up – usually with a nice cup of tea.

The servants do their best to teach the Beast how to behave.

Pointy spout

Likes: Serving a spot of tea, giving advice, making guests feel at home in the castle

Dislikes: Bad manners, dirty china, bad tempers

Dream: To become human again

The Beast knew that Belle may be his only chance of finding true love. Mrs Potts, the helpful teapot, told the Beast that if he wanted Belle to see past his scary looks, he should be kind to her and learn to control his fiery temper. The Beast tried to act like a gentleman by politely asking Belle to join him for dinner. But when she refused, he ordered the servants to make sure that she did not leave her room for the rest of the night. He decided that if she would not eat with him, then she would not eat at all!

After a little while, Belle decided to go against the Beast's wishes and explore her new home. When she found the kitchen, she met the enchanted servants, including Mrs Potts' son, Chip, who thought Belle was very pretty. The servants did everything they could to show Belle that she was not just a prisoner, but their guest. They even prepared a wonderful feast in her honour. Lumière and Cogsworth wanted Belle to feel at home in the castle, so they offered to give her a tour. Belle happily accepted – it was her first time in an enchanted castle, after all!

Chip

Cheerful Chip loves doing tricks and telling stories. This curious little teacup likes to know what is going on and loves meeting new people. When he isn't helping Mrs Potts, he is always looking for someone to play with.

Chipped rim

Dinner is also a show!

Likes: Making new friends, telling stories

Dislikes: Going to bed early, taking baths, sleeping in the cupboard, being left out

Favourite trick: Blowing bubbles in tea!

The Beast

The hot-tempered Beast knows he is scary to look at. He hides himself away in his castle, using only a magic mirror to see the outside world. He does not think that anyone could love him.

While Belle was exploring with Lumière and Cogsworth, she wandered into the West Wing. This was the only place that the Beast had forbidden her from going. Belle was curious about what was hidden in there, so she decided to look around. Just as she found the rose that had been left by the enchantress, the Beast suddenly appeared! He angrily shouted at her to get out. Belle was so frightened that she ran away from the castle.

Sharp, scary fangs

The Beast will not let Belle near the enchanted rose.

Dream: To find someone to love him, despite his terrifying appearance

Likes: Staying in his castle, looking into his magic mirror

Dislikes: His reflection, being disobeyed

Belle rode Phillipe through the forest but a fierce wolf pack attacked them. The Beast rushed to help, and saved Belle's life, but he was hurt. Belle took the Beast back to the castle to help him recover. She thanked the Beast for saving her but told him that he had to learn to control his temper. She was finally beginning to see that he was not as scary as he looked. The servants, including Wardrobe and Featherduster, were pleased to see the start of a new friendship.

The wolves are no match for the Beast's strength.

Featherduster and Wardrobe

These two castle helpers are eager to do whatever it takes to help romance blossom for the Beast and Belle – from making the castle gleam to providing the perfect dress.

Feather "skirt"

Bright red lips

The Beast can be rude, but Belle always sticks up for herself.

Likes: Singing, pretty dresses, having fun, helping the Beast, keeping the castle spotless

Dislikes: Not being able to wear their human clothes anymore

A new beginning

Belle may be staying in the castle out of duty, but that doesn't mean she'll pout and mope. She knows there is always joy to be found – sometimes in surprising places!

Belle has never seen so many books before!

Hair tied in pretty bow

Comfortable green dress

The Beast was determined to make a fresh start with Belle. He wanted to do something kind for her, to show her how much she meant to him. He surprised Belle by showing her the huge castle library, promising that it was hers from now on. Belle was amazed – it was the nicest thing anyone had ever done for her. She now had enough books to last a lifetime! She offered to teach the Beast how to read so that he could share her greatest passion with her.

As time went by, Belle and the Beast began to spend more time together. As they ate delicious meals and played in the snow,

The Beast shows that he does have a gentle side.

they both realised how much they liked being with each other. Belle was the first person to really make the Beast smile. As their friendship blossomed, Belle could finally see the good inside the Beast. She realised that he was not as bad-tempered as she had thought. He was sweet and gentle, and she knew she could trust him. The servants watched the happy pair with delight, and everyone seemed happier.

Fun in the castle

Belle has a gift for finding great joy in simple things – from feeding the little birds around the castle, to playing in the snow and, of course, diving into one of her favourite books!

Fur-lined cloak to keep warm

Matching pink dress

Monsieur D'Arque

Scheming Monsieur D'Arque will do anything for gold, even harm people. However, sometimes it seems that he causes trouble just for the fun of it.

Gaston knows that Monsieur D'Arque will do anything he asks, if he gives him enough gold.

Long, grey hair

Likes: Evil plots

Dislikes: Anyone who gets in his way

Goal: To make lots of money. He will agree to any dirty plan, as long as there is a reward involved.

Meanwhile, Maurice tried to convince the townsfolk that Belle had been kidnapped by the Beast. But they just laughed at him – they still thought he was crazy. This gave Gaston a terrible idea. He paid the wicked owner of the insane asylum, Monsieur D'Arque, to lock Maurice away. Gaston would offer to free Maurice, but only if Belle agreed to marry him. Gaston was sure that she would do anything for her father and would not refuse him this time! But before Gaston could do anything, Maurice left to search for Belle alone.

Back at the castle, Belle and the Beast shared a romantic evening, dancing in the grand ballroom. The Beast planned to tell Belle that he loved her, but before he could, Belle told him that she wished she could see her father again. The Beast would do anything to make Belle happy, so he told her she could see her father in his magic mirror. When she did, she saw that Maurice was lost in the woods and very sick. The Beast let Belle go, giving her the mirror to take with her, so that she always had a way to look back and remember him.

Belle of the ball

Graceful Belle glows with joy as she waltzes through the grand ballroom. She doesn't yet know that there's a prince within the Beast – all she knows is that her heart is filled with love.

Elegant hairstyle

Delicate, evening gloves

Stunning satin ballgown

Belle and the Beast share a dance to remember.

The angry mob

Gaston convinces the townsfolk that the Beast is a dangerous monster. They will not rest until they have stormed his castle and defeated him!

Armed for battle

Belle found Maurice and took him home to look after him. But soon there was a knock at the door – Monsieur D'Arque had come to take Maurice to the asylum! Quick-thinking Belle proved that her father had been telling the truth, by using the magic mirror to show the townsfolk that the Beast was real. But Gaston then persuaded the others that they should hunt

An enchanted coatrack helps to defend the castle from attack.

and kill the Beast, and he led an angry mob of townsfolk to the castle. The Beast's loyal servants fought back bravely and defeated the mob. However, Gaston was able to sneak past them and attack the Beast! The Beast was so unhappy without Belle that he did not even try to fight back.

Leaders: Gaston and Lefou

Goal: To protect their town by destroying the Beast

Weapons: Torches, pitchforks – anything they can get their hands on

The Beast begins to transform.

Human again

Released from the spell at last, the Prince's true form emerges. Now, filled with love for Belle and affection for his servants, the handsome Prince is ready to rule over a very happy household.

Long, soft hair

Warm smile

Belle rushed to save the Beast. When he saw that she had returned to him, the Beast began to fight back. He managed to defeat Gaston, but he was badly hurt. Belle feared she was too late and confessed her love for him. The spell was broken just as the last petal fell from the enchanted rose. The Beast changed into a handsome prince! At first Belle did not recognise him, but when she gazed into his eyes, she saw that he was her beloved Beast. The curse was lifted from the castle, and Belle and her Prince celebrated with a magnificent ball.

Jewelled headband

Magic lamp

Elegant shawl

Aladdin

Far away in the kingdom of Agrabah,
strict laws separated rich from poor, and a
lonely princess from a lowly street rat. But
just under the desert lay a powerful magic
waiting to be unlocked…and ready
to change Jasmine's world.

Contents

Aladdin

Aladdin is a "diamond in the rough". On the outside he wears shabby, patched clothes, but inside he has the heart and courage of a prince.

Life in the desert city of Agrabah was hard for Aladdin, a smart, streetwise street urchin. He had no parents, no money and no job. He spent his days stealing food and dodging trouble. People called him a thief and a street

Aladdin can usually outrun the Royal Guards, but sometimes they catch up.

rat, but Aladdin was simply poor and hungry, and he only stole to survive. He knew that he was more than just a thief and he hoped to be able to show people the real Aladdin some day.

Loose pants

Aladdin has a kind heart.

Home: High on a rooftop in Agrabah – he has the best view in the city

Likes: Having fun, helping others

Dislikes: Being poor, being called a street rat, people thinking that he has fleas

He was often in trouble, but Aladdin was also brave and kind. He would always help anyone in need – from hungry children to beautiful princesses. Aladdin lived on a dusty rooftop with his best pal, Abu the monkey. Their home had a great view of the Sultan's palace and Aladdin used to gaze at it and dream of being as rich as the Sultan.

Aladdin dreams of living in a palace just like the Sultan's.

Anyone who lived in a palace must be rich and happy, with no problems – right?

Abu

Small, mischievous and an expert thief, Abu is the perfect pet for Aladdin. However, unlike Aladdin, Abu really enjoys stealing things, especially shiny jewels.

Abu loves honey

Same type of vest as Aladdin

Aladdin and Abu stick together through thick and thin!

Best friend: Aladdin

Favourite food: Juicy watermelons

Likes: Food, shiny objects, tricking market vendors, causing trouble for the guards

Dislikes: Being in danger

Jasmine

Jasmine is not sure that she really likes being a princess. She has never even stepped outside the palace walls. Jasmine longs for adventure and excitement.

Jasmine longs to be free like a bird.

Long, flowing hair

Gold jewellery

Dream: To see the world beyond the palace walls

Best friend: Her pet tiger, Rajah – she tells him all of her secrets and dreams

Dislikes: Arrogant suitors, being told what to do

Princess Jasmine lived in Agrabah's palace with her father, the Sultan. However, she was far from happy. Jasmine had all the fine clothes and delicious food that a girl could ever desire, but she felt trapped and frustrated. There was so much of the world that she had never even seen. An ancient law decreed that she must choose a prince to marry before her next birthday, but Jasmine hated being told what to do. When she married, she wanted it to be for love, not because of a law.

The Sultan loved his daughter and he was a good man, but he wanted her to obey the law and get married. He knew that he wouldn't be around to protect her forever. He hoped she would find a kind and brave prince who would take care of her…if she would only let him! So far, Jasmine had rejected every suitor that her father had suggested. With her birthday in just three days, time was running out fast and the Sultan was beginning to despair.

Sultan

The Sultan is a simple man. He thinks that everyone should just be nice and follow the law. If they did that, he would have more time for puzzles and taking Magic Carpet rides!

Bushy beard

Jasmine wants to marry for love, but her father is worried about the law.

Home: A magnificent palace in Agrabah

Likes: Playing with his toy animals, watching parades

Dislikes: Jasmine rejecting perfectly decent princes – her mother wasn't nearly as picky!

Jafar

Devious Jafar flatters the Sultan and pretends to serve him, but he is actually planning to destroy him. Jafar doesn't care about anyone – he just wants to be the most powerful person in Agrabah.

Long, red robes

Snake staff

The Sultan's advisor thinks he would be a better ruler.

Job: Royal vizier (official advisor)

Goal: To rule over Agrabah

Likes: Being in control, getting his own way

Powers: He can hypnotise people into doing his bidding

While the Sultan spent his days worrying about Jasmine's future, he left his trusted vizier, Jafar, in charge of Agrabah. Unfortunately, Jafar was a wicked man who had been using his magical serpent staff to hypnotise the Sultan into doing whatever he wanted. Jafar was secretly plotting to overthrow the Sultan and had heard about a magic lamp that might help him. He was determined to do whatever it took to find it.

Only one creature knew Jafar's true personality – his pet parrot, Iago. The talkative bird was certainly no ordinary animal. In fact, he was just as wicked as his master and had a few cunning ideas of his own. While Jafar and Iago plotted to take the Sultan's place, Jasmine had come up with a daring plan. She was going to run away from the palace and seek out a new life, where she could do whatever she chose.

Iago

Iago is a rude and impatient bird. He hates having to pretend to like the Sultan. He can't wait for the day that Jafar rules Agrabah, as long as Iago is by his master's side, of course.

Blue-tipped feathers

Sharp claws

Jafar's feathery assistant is always ready to whisper advice and encouragement into his master's ear.

Abilities: Mimicking voices

Likes: Helping Jafar carry out his evil plans, insulting people whenever they can't hear him

Dislikes: The Sultan stuffing bird food into his beak – Polly does not want a cracker!

Rajah

Rajah is a gentle, playful tiger, but he is also very strong. He is protective of Jasmine. He has been known to scare away princes who only want to marry her for her wealth and status.

Long whiskers

Thick, soft fur

Likes: Cheering up Jasmine, playing in the gardens, being petted

Dislikes: Being left alone, strangers

Favourite game: Chasing away pesky suitors – he always tries to rip off their trousers!

When Rajah saw that Jasmine was about to escape, he tried to stop her. However, when Jasmine explained why she had to leave, Rajah understood. He even helped his friend climb over the palace wall. Outside the palace, Jasmine was excited by the noisy, busy world, but she didn't know how to behave there in order to fit in. When she saw a hungry child, she gave him an apple from a nearby market stall without paying for it. Suddenly she was being called a thief!

A tiger makes a good bodyguard.

Clever disguise

No one in the market knows that Jasmine is a princess, especially when she is wearing a simple brown robe and hood. She feels free at last and doesn't plan on going home. Ever.

Aladdin saves Jasmine just in time.

Aladdin couldn't help noticing the beautiful young woman in the market place. When he saw that she was in trouble, he decided to help. Thinking quickly, he told the stall owner that Jasmine was his sister and that she was a little crazy. Jasmine played along and managed to escape with Aladdin to his rooftop home. The princess and the street urchin discovered that they had a lot in common, until they were rudely interrupted…

Jasmine is fascinated by Aladdin's adventurous life.

Royal headdress is hidden

Long, brown robe

Brown, pointy shoes

Razoul

Mean and menacing Razoul enjoys working for Jafar. He never questions his master's orders – he just follows them. He only wishes his guards were as clever as he thinks he is!

Uniform of the Royal Guards

Jafar had discovered that Aladdin was the only person who could help him find the magic lamp, so he sent his guards to find the boy. Led by the terrifying Captain Razoul, the guards were under orders to take Aladdin to Jafar. Aladdin tried to run, but the guards were too strong for him. Jasmine even revealed her true identity to try and save her new friend, but Razoul would answer only to Jafar.

Razoul and the guards catch Aladdin and drag him off to the dungeon.

Razoul is surprised to find Jasmine outside the palace.

Job: Captain of the Guard

Master: Jafar – Razoul carries out his master's dirty deeds.

Dislikes: Street rats, troublemakers, being outsmarted, anyone who gets in his way

Aladdin was thrown in jail, but Jafar told Jasmine he was dead. Aladdin couldn't stop thinking about the princess. He was falling in love with her, but she would never be allowed to marry a street rat like him. However, a strange old prisoner offered to help Aladdin escape if he would just go with him to a magical treasure cave. Aladdin quickly agreed – he hoped that he would find enough treasure to convince the Sultan to let him marry Jasmine!

A strange old man

This mysterious elderly prisoner seems too good to be true – and he is. He is really Jafar in disguise! He doesn't want to help Aladdin. He only wants to find the magic lamp.

Long, white beard

Missing teeth

Tattered robe

The elderly man is too frail to go to the cave by himself – or so Aladdin believes.

Cave of Wonders

The Cave of Wonders is a powerful being who will only allow a "diamond in the rough" to claim the magic lamp. However, it will punish anyone who tries to take its other treasures.

The Cave holds piles of treasure.

Entrance to the Cave

Abilities: Stopping those who are unworthy of entering, trapping visitors who try to take the treasure

Dislikes: Being disturbed or disobeyed, greedy people who cannot resist temptation

Still disguised as an old man, Jafar led Aladdin and his friend Abu to the Cave of Wonders in the middle of the desert. Sure enough, the Cave gave Aladdin permission to enter, as long as he did not touch anything except the lamp. While Jafar waited outside, Aladdin and Abu nervously entered the Cave. It was filled with mountains of gold and precious jewels, which could have made Aladdin and Abu rich beyond their wildest dreams. But there was no sign of the lamp.

Aladdin and Abu searched through the vast Cave and met a shy Magic Carpet. Luckily the enchanted Carpet knew exactly where the magic lamp was. However, just as Aladdin collected the lamp, Abu couldn't resist snatching an enormous ruby. The Cave was angry that its rule had been broken. It tried to trap Aladdin and Abu, but the Carpet came to their rescue. Aladdin handed the lamp to Jafar, and the evil vizier tried to give him his "eternal reward" – death! Abu managed to stop Jafar by biting his arm, and stole the magic lamp back!

The Magic Carpet enjoys teasing Abu, but Aladdin's friend is not amused.

Magic Carpet

The Magic Carpet is very clever. It is eager to help Aladdin and Abu, even though it is quite nervous. It hopes that they can all become good friends.

Tassels work like hands

Likes: Flying, sneaking up on people, making new friends, helping people who come to the Cave

Dislikes: Being in the Cave for too long, getting trampled on

Favourite game: Chess

Genie

The Genie is powerful, kind and a little bit crazy. He can do just about anything, except bring people back to life, make people fall in love or free himself from the lamp!

Gold cuff on each wrist

Only three fingers

Dream: To finally be free from his lamp

Likes: Helping Aladdin, having fun, doing impressions

Powers: He can grant three wishes to each master – no more, no less!

Aladdin and Abu were still trapped inside the Cave, but were safe from Jafar for now. Aladdin could not understand what was so special about the lamp, until he rubbed it.

A Genie appeared and told Aladdin that he would grant him three wishes! Aladdin thought carefully about his wishes, but first, he tricked the Genie into freeing him from the Cave. Aladdin promised to free the Genie with his final wish, but his first wish was to be turned into a prince.

Genie loves to entertain his master, Aladdin.

Prince Ali makes an
impressive entrance.

Prince Ali

Aladdin does not believe
that he is good enough
for Jasmine, but he thinks
that Prince Ali is. He plans
to be confident and charming
to win her heart.

Clothes
fit for a
prince

Pointy
boots

That was no problem for the Genie. Soon Aladdin was transformed into the dashing Prince Ali, and Abu into his trusty elephant. Street urchin Aladdin might not be able to marry Princess Jasmine, but surely the wealthy and sophisticated Prince Ali could? With the Genie's help, Prince Ali set off to win his bride in style. However, he had overlooked one important fact – Jasmine had already fallen in love with Aladdin.

Strong will

Jasmine is delighted that Aladdin is alive, but angry that he has tricked her by pretending to be a prince. She is tired of other people deciding what is good or bad for her!

Jasmine and Aladdin are so high in the sky they can touch the clouds.

More formal, purple outfit

Jewel matches headdress

When Jasmine met Prince Ali, she thought that he was another arrogant prince and rejected him. However, he persuaded her to take a ride on the Magic Carpet and Jasmine finally realised that Prince Ali was the boy from the market. But Aladdin still couldn't admit the truth – he told her that he was a prince all along. It seemed that Jasmine had finally found love, but Jafar was determined that Prince Ali would not spoil his plans to be Sultan. Prince Ali had to be removed.

Jasmine knows that Aladdin is the man she has been waiting for.

Evil Jafar had Aladdin thrown into the ocean. The Genie managed to save Aladdin, but this used up his second wish. To Jafar's surprise, Aladdin returned to the palace unharmed. The vizier was furious…until he spotted the lamp on Prince Ali's belt and worked out his true identity. Jafar sent Iago to steal the lamp, and when it was finally in his possession, Jafar's first wish was to be Sultan.

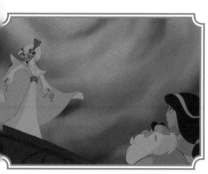

Jafar uses his new magical powers to declare himself the new Sultan.

The Genie had no choice but to grant that wish, and his second one – to be the most powerful sorcerer in the world. Now Jafar had the power to banish Aladdin and make Jasmine, the Sultan and Rajah his slaves.

Slave princess

Jasmine can't think of a worse fate than having to do what Jafar wants. She decides to play along. She hopes that Aladdin has a plan to get them all out of this terrible situation.

Long, gold earrings

Red outfit chosen by Jafar

Wrists kept in chains

Ultimate power

Jafar's biggest weakness is his own ego. He is so busy trying to be powerful that he allows himself to be defeated by a mere street rat. He does not realise Aladdin's real plans until it is too late.

Jafar thought he had finally got rid of Aladdin, but he was wrong. With a little help from Abu and the Magic Carpet, Aladdin came back to rescue Jasmine. When Jafar wished for Jasmine to fall in love with him, the princess pretended it had worked. Meanwhile, Aladdin tried to steal the lamp back. Unfortunately he failed, and Jafar trapped Jasmine in an hourglass. Then Jafar turned himself into a giant snake and attacked Aladdin. However, Aladdin was too clever for Jafar.

Sharp, black claws

Jafar's genie beard

Jafar's genie form

When Jafar is in his snakelike form, he can use his long body to trap Aladdin, and his sharp teeth to bite him!

He told Jafar that the Genie was more powerful than him, so Jafar decided to use his third wish to become a genie, so that he could rule the universe. When the Genie granted this wish, Aladdin trapped Jafar in a lamp and freed Jasmine. He used his own final wish to free the Genie. Jasmine's

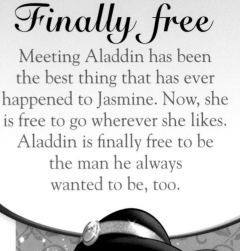

Genie's gold cuffs magically disappear when Aladdin grants him his freedom.

father changed the law so Jasmine could marry anyone she chose. Of course, she chose Aladdin.

Finally free

Meeting Aladdin has been the best thing that has ever happened to Jasmine. Now, she is free to go wherever she likes. Aladdin is finally free to be the man he always wanted to be, too.

Sparkling jewels

Shimmering skirt

Delicate, pointy blue shoes

Nothing can keep the happy couple apart.

Flowing,
black hair

Decorative
jewels

Fringed
hem

Pocahontas

When settlers arrived on the shores of the New World, free-spirited Pocahontas and a daring explorer had a lot to learn from each other. Together, they hoped to save their people and bring lasting peace to the land.

Contents

John Smith

John is brave, kind and willing to risk his life for others. He thinks that building roads and houses will help the people of the New World have better lives.

John can't wait to start his big adventure in the New World.

Sword to fight "savages"

Home: London, England

Likes: Travelling, exploring, having adventures, meeting new people, trying new things

Dislikes: Staying in one place for too long when there's so much of the world to see!

In 1607, America was a little-known place called the New World. Many people had heard that there was gold to be found there. They wanted to search for it and become very rich. They didn't stop to think about the people who lived there. They thought those people were "savages". Explorer John Smith had been on many voyages around the world. However, his real passion was adventure, not gold. He hoped that his latest mission, as captain of the ship named *Susan Constant*, would be his greatest adventure yet.

Chief Powhatan

Chief Powhatan is a fearless warrior, wise leader and loving father. He has to make difficult decisions, but he is fair. He always does what he believes to be right.

For many years, a tribe in the New World had lived in harmony with the earth. They respected nature and were proud of their beautiful homeland. The tribe's Chief was a wise and respected leader. He cared a lot about the safety of his people and was prepared to go to war to protect them. Chief Powhatan had one beloved daughter, Pocahontas. His greatest wish was for her to be happy. He believed that the right path for her was marriage to a strong man from the tribe.

Feathered headdress

Buckskin cape

Chief Powhatan returns to his people after winning a battle with a rival tribe.

Job: Chief of the tribe

Dream: For Pocahontas to marry a strong warrior

Goal: To keep his tribe safe from intruders, so that they may live in peace

Pocahontas

Pocahontas is strong, wise and independent. She is determined to follow her heart. She hopes that it will lead her down an exciting and adventurous path.

Pocahontas was a fun-loving young woman with a free spirit, just like her mother before her. Pocahontas often wandered far from her tribe in search of new adventures. She felt happiest when she was close to nature, paddling down rivers, exploring woods and diving off waterfalls. She loved her father and wanted to please him. But in her heart, Pocahontas believed that he had chosen the wrong path for her. She often dreamed of a spinning arrow and felt sure that it was a clue to her true destiny.

Necklace belonged to Pocahontas's mother

Traditional dress

Pocahontas thinks she is like a river – free and unpredictable.

Dream: To follow her own path

Likes: Nature, going wherever the wind takes her, thinking about her dreams

Dislikes: War, not being allowed to make her own choices

Kocoum is a great warrior, but he is always so serious and finds it hard to show his emotions.

Kocoum

Kocoum might not show it, but he loves Pocahontas. He hopes that one day she will return his feelings and marry him. Until then he plans to do everything he can to protect her.

Feather in hair

Painted bear paws represent courage

Kocoum, the strongest and most fearless warrior in the tribe, had asked Chief Powhatan's permission to marry Pocahontas. The Chief was delighted – he thought Kocoum would make a fine husband for his daughter. But even though Kocoum was handsome and heroic, Pocahontas was not in love with him. She thought he was too serious – he never smiled or wanted to play games. In fact, he hardly even spoke! Pocahontas told her father how she felt, but the Chief hoped that she would soon change her mind.

Abilities: Has the strength of a bear – no one has ever defeated him!

Likes: Serving his tribe, leading his fellow warriors to great victories

Dislikes: Threats to the tribe

Governor Ratcliffe

Governor Ratcliffe is not a popular man. He is lazy, selfish and a complete failure. He hopes that his latest voyage will change his fortunes.

Hair tied in red ribbons

Map of the New World

Dream: To impress King James by settling in the New World, taking gold from the Indians

Likes: Gold, ordering his men around, power, getting revenge

Dislikes: Hard work, being humiliated, "savages"

Meanwhile, the *Susan Constant* had finally arrived in the New World. The voyage was paid for by a man named Governor Ratcliffe. He was mean, nasty and greedy. Ratcliffe was desperate to find gold in the New World. He hoped that he could return to England as a very rich man so that everyone would have to respect him. Ratcliffe ordered his crew to inspect the land and make sure that the "savages" did not get in their way. As soon as he knew that the land was safe, he too would go ashore.

Ratcliffe is determined to find the gold – as long as his men do all the hard work!

John and his crew are happy to finally get off the ship and onto dry land.

John Smith led the crew ashore, and Pocahontas watched as they surveyed the land. She was careful not to be seen, but her

Pocahontas secretly observes the crew from behind a rock.

curious raccoon friend, Meeko, went straight up to John! The explorer had never seen anything like it before. He offered the raccoon a tasty biscuit and greedy Meeko gobbled it down. Pretty soon he was good friends with the kind explorer. John suspected that Meeko was not alone, but before he could discover Pocahontas, he had to return to his crew.

Meeko thinks anyone with delicious food can't be dangerous.

Meeko

Meeko the raccoon is a curious creature. He loves exploring with Pocahontas, especially when he discovers tasty treats. Meeko has a huge appetite and he is always hungry!

Tasty biscuit

Stripy, bushy tail

Favourite food: Biscuits

Best friend: Pocahontas

Likes: Teasing Flit the hummingbird, finding shiny treasures, eating whatever he can get his paws on

Kekata

Kekata is a skilled healer. He also understands Pocahontas better than her father. He sees that Pocahontas is strong, wise and free, just like her mother was.

Long, grey hair

Healing kit

While Pocahontas was watching the new arrivals with interest, her tribespeople were worried. Kekata, the tribe's spiritual healer, was wary of the strange men. He warned the tribespeople that they had "weapons that spout fire and thunder". Kocoum in particular was eager to start a war. But the wise Chief ordered him to watch the strangers first, and find out as much as he could about them. The Chief hoped that the visitors did not plan to stay long.

Chief Powhatan tells his people not to make any hasty decisions.

Job: The village's healer

Abilities: Interpreting dreams, healing the sick and wounded, making predictions

Dislikes: Greedy settlers with strange weapons

Bossy Governor Ratcliffe pushes his men to keep on digging. It is the only way to find the gold.

Ben and Lon

Crew members and good friends Ben and Lon are hard workers who don't mind digging holes at first. However, when they fail to find anything and begin to run out of food, they begin to lose faith in Ratcliffe.

Unfortunately, Ratcliffe was going to stay as long as it took to collect every last piece of gold. He set his crew, including Ben and Lon, to work, chopping down trees and digging holes. He didn't care about the land or nature – he just wanted his riches. Little did he know that no matter how long his crew spent digging, they wouldn't find anything. There was no gold in the New World! However, one crew member hadn't come to dig holes. John Smith had come for adventure.

Scruffy, red beard

Leather waistcoat

Job: Sailors for the Virginia Company

Dream: To make their fortunes overseas by finding gold

Role model: John Smith – they've heard amazing tales about his adventures

Flit

Flit is a tiny hummingbird with a big personality and a sharp beak. He is very feisty and he will do anything to protect his friend Pocahontas. He also loves annoying his pal Meeko.

John Smith and Pocahontas have a lot to learn from each other.

Pink chin

Long, sharp beak

Feathery tail

Likes: Looking out for Pocahontas, playing pranks, pecking at people with his beak whenever they are being annoying

Dislikes: Strangers, Meeko being silly

While John was exploring the New World, he felt someone watching him. Sensing danger, he raised his gun. But then he saw that it was a beautiful young woman. John had never seen anyone as lovely as Pocahontas before. He wanted to talk to her, but she ran away. John followed and begged Pocahontas to stay with him. Somehow Pocahontas sensed that she could trust this stranger, although her friend Flit wasn't so sure!

Suspicious Flit is not so trusting of the stranger, but Meeko keeps him under control.

Pocahontas and John were fascinated by each other and soon grew closer. Unfortunately, the tribespeople and the crew were also getting to know each other – and they were far less friendly. When the crew spotted the tribe, they began firing guns at them. In the heat of battle, young Thomas tripped over and

Thomas is young and inexperienced in battle.

accidentally fired his gun. His shot just missed Ratcliffe. When one of the warriors in the tribe was wounded, they ran back to their village to send for reinforcements. A war seemed very likely to happen.

Thomas

Thomas is not a very good sailor or soldier. He nearly drowned on the voyage to the New World, but John saved him. Thomas owes him his life and has vowed to pay him back some day.

Sailor's cap

Dream: To get a huge pile of gold and build himself a big house in the New World

Likes: Making friends, doing what is right

Dislikes: Ratcliffe's temper and arrogance

Kocoum rushes to rescue the injured tribesman.

Nakoma

Nakoma has been Pocahontas's best friend since they were children. They are extremely close, even though they are nothing like each other. Nakoma is quiet and sensible, while Pocahontas is bold and rebellious.

Hair tied back with leather string

John told Pocahontas all about England. He showed her his compass, explaining that the arrow could help you find the right path if you were lost. In turn, Pocahontas showed John that just because her life was very different to his, it didn't mean that she was a "savage". However, Pocahontas soon had to return to her village. There, her friend Nakoma sensed that she was hiding something. When she found out that Pocahontas was friends with one of the settlers, she was shocked. But she agreed to keep her friend's secret. For now.

Nakoma is afraid Pocahontas is going to get hurt.

Likes: Helping her tribe, playing and being silly with Pocahontas, gazing at the handsome Kocoum

Dislikes: Breaking the rules, getting into trouble, being ignored by Pocahontas

John told his crew there was no gold and that they should make friends with the tribe. The crew,

Both Meeko and Percy hate all of the fighting.

including Ratcliffe's dog, Percy, were tired of fighting. They began to wonder if John was right. But Ratcliffe didn't believe him – he wanted a fight. John sneaked out to warn Pocahontas, not realising that Thomas was following him. Meanwhile, Nakoma had revealed Pocahontas's secret to Kocoum. When the warrior found her with John, he jealously attacked him. Thomas tried to save his friend by shooting Kocoum.

John tries to defend himself, but he is no match for jealous Kocoum.

Percy

Percy is Governor Ratcliffe's spoiled pet pug. He is pampered and lazy, until he meets Meeko. After a rocky start, the pug and raccoon become best pals and bond over their shared love of food.

Fancy collar with gold medallion

Likes: Doggie treats, being carried around on his own velvet cushion, being spoilt and pampered

Dislikes: Being bothered by Meeko, getting dirty, not getting what he wants

Grandmother Willow

Grandmother Willow is a wise and ancient willow tree. She offers Pocahontas advice whenever she needs it. Grandmother Willow understands that Pocahontas loves John and can see that he is a good man.

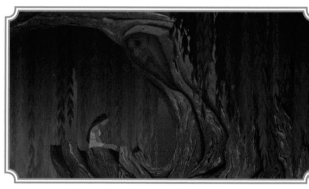

Pocahontas turns to wise Grandmother Willow for comfort after John's capture.

Kocoum was killed! John knew that Chief Powhatan would execute Thomas, so he took the blame himself, and was sentenced to death. Pocahontas was heartbroken, but John didn't have any regrets. He was just glad to have met her.

Pocahontas turned to Grandmother Willow for advice. She helped her realise that the arrow on John's compass was the arrow from her dreams. He was her true path – she had to save him! Unfortunately, Ratcliffe was on his way to attack the tribe.

Face appears in the old tree

Abilities: Great wisdom that she has gained over hundreds of years. She can also use her branches to whip and trip up anyone who bothers her.

Likes: Helping Pocahontas

Dislikes: Fighting, ignorance

Just before the Chief was to kill John, Pocahontas begged her father to choose peace. Finally, he saw that she was right and declared that the fighting should stop. Ratcliffe had no intention of listening and he fired at the Chief. John blocked the bullet, and was badly wounded. The whole crew turned against Ratcliffe – even his valet,

John risked his own life to protect Chief Powhatan.

Wiggins. John had to return to England to get well again. Pocahontas was very sad, but she knew her tribe needed her to stay. She promised that John Smith would always be in her heart.

Pocahontas waves goodbye to John.

Wiggins

Wiggins is a good valet. He works hard, always listens to his boss and never criticises. However, even he has to admit that Ratcliffe is a truly terrible leader.

Valet's yellow uniform

Job: Governor Ratcliffe's valet

Likes: Decorating, trimming bushes into amazing animal shapes, making lovely gift baskets

Dislikes: Fighting, upsetting people

Silk
sleeves

Traditional
outfit

Delicate
embroidery

Mulan

Long ago in China, the only
way for a girl to bring honour to her
family was to be a graceful lady and a
dutiful bride. Mulan would need all
of her courage to break free from
tradition, save China and still be
true to her heart.

Contents

Mulan

Young Mulan wants to bring honour to her family, but she wishes that she could do it in her own way. She is not a quiet, delicate lady. She is full of energy and bursting with ideas.

In Ancient China, sons were brought up to be brave soldiers. Daughters were expected to bring honour and good fortune to their families by finding good husbands and being loyal wives. Fa Mulan was the only daughter in her traditional Chinese family. She loved her family very much and wanted to make them proud of her, but she always seemed to be making a mess of things. She was not graceful or obedient. She was clumsy, always late and a little bit forgetful. No matter how hard Mulan tried, she could never master the art of being an elegant lady.

Traditional Chinese robe

Mulan paints notes on her arm to remind her to be graceful.

Likes: Spending time with her family, being herself, new challenges

Dislikes: Girls being treated differently to boys

Dream: To bring honour to the Fa family

Mulan gets Little Brother to help with the chores.

Little Brother

Little Brother will do anything he can to help Mulan. He loves her even more than a juicy bone, although he hopes that he will never have to choose between the two!

Mulan's best friend was Little Brother, who was actually a small dog. Little Brother enjoyed helping Mulan with her chores, such as feeding the chickens and the family horse. However, just like his owner, Little Brother had a habit of creating chaos without meaning to. One particular day, Mulan needed even more help than usual. She was off to meet the village Matchmaker to show her that she would make a good bride. She was quite nervous and, of course, she was running late.

Sometimes helping with chores can lead to a bit of a mess.

Alert ears

Likes: Running around the garden, being silly with Mulan, feeding the animals, playing with the chickens

Favourite food: Tasty bones – he will help Mulan with any chore if he can have one as a reward!

Fa Zhou

Fa Zhou is a proud, dutiful man. As a soldier, he fought bravely for China and was injured in battle. He will now do anything to protect the honour of his family – even if he has to risk his life.

Fa Zhou prays to his ancestors

Walking stick

Values: Loyalty, courage, honour

Job: He was once a great war hero, but has now retired

Favourite place: Under the blossom tree in his garden. He loves sitting there with Mulan.

Mulan's parents loved their daughter, but they often worried about her. Mulan's father, Fa Zhou, had been a famous soldier, but now he was old and not very well. Every day, he prayed to his ancestors, asking them to help Mulan impress the Matchmaker and bring honour to the Fa family.

Fa Zhou always believes in his daughter. But she can be so clumsy sometimes!

Fa Zhou believed in his daughter, but he thought that a good marriage was the only way she could help her family.

Mulan's mother, Fa Li, shared her husband's concerns. If Mulan did not make a good impression on the Matchmaker, she did not know what would happen to the family. Mulan would never make a good marriage, and they would all be disgraced. Her daughter was late as usual, so Fa Li wished that she had prayed to the Ancestors, too – for luck! Eventually, Mulan arrived, but before she could meet the Matchmaker, she had to be bathed, groomed and dressed properly for the occasion.

Looking elegant is the only way to impress the Matchmaker.

Fa Li

Fa Li worries for her daughter. She sees that Mulan is not happy, but she thinks that she will be fine just as long as she can find a good husband. It is just the way things are.

Hair tied in a traditional knot

Likes: Upholding traditions, taking care of her family, Mulan behaving herself

Greatest fear: That Mulan will not make a good marriage

Strengths: She always has great patience.

Grandmother Fa

Grandmother Fa wants to help Mulan impress the Matchmaker because she thinks that traditions are important. However, the strong-willed old lady actually has a lot in common with her feisty granddaughter.

Grandmother thinks it is important to test Cri-Kee's luck.

Very long ears

Mulan's Grandmother agreed with Fa Li that Mulan needed a little luck. She found a lucky cricket, Cri-Kee, and tested his powers by crossing a busy road with her eyes closed. When she survived the daring stunt without a scratch, Grandmother decided that Cri-Kee was indeed very lucky. However, Grandmother Fa thought that even Cri-Kee might not be enough to help Mulan make a good impression on the Matchmaker. She also gave Mulan an apple for serenity, a pendant for balance and some jade beads for beauty.

Likes: Handsome young men, speaking her mind, helping Mulan

Favourite colour: Jade green

Beliefs: Carrying the right special object or animal can help you get through any tricky situation

Mulan has a last-minute practice.

Cri-Kee

Cri-Kee always likes to know what is happening, but he often ends up a little too close for comfort. Thankfully, one of his friends is usually around to save him. He must be lucky after all!

Long, pointy antennae

Grandmother was confident that luck was on their side and that Mulan's meeting with the Matchmaker would be a success, but Cri-Kee was not so sure.

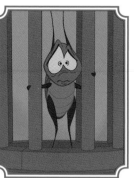

Cri-Kee wants to help. First, he has to get out of his cage.

Grandmother had had her eyes covered, but Cri-Kee had seen the chaos she had brought to the busy road! He was supposed to stay in the cage Grandmother had attached to Mulan's robe, but he wanted to be closer to the action.

Job: Mulan's lucky charm – although he is not sure if he really is lucky!

Likes: Being helpful, taking a nice bath in a warm cup of tea

Dislikes: Getting squashed, staying still

Elegant lady

Mulan tries so hard to impress the Matchmaker, but she is not being her real self. She doesn't want to disappoint her father. But how can she find a way to bring honour to her family and be true to herself?

Mulan was eager to please the Matchmaker. She had learned to recite a set of rules called the Final Admonition, practised pouring tea, and, for once, was dressed like an elegant lady. The Matchmaker would test her on many things, and if she failed, Mulan would never be able to find a good husband. As she waited with four other nervous young women, Mulan hoped that her ancestors would guide her so that she did not make a fool of herself. Sadly, the Matchmaker immediately noticed Mulan.

Beautiful paper fan

Graceful and poised

Fashionably long sleeves

Traditional long train

The beautiful young women try to impress the Matchmaker.

Matchmaker

The Matchmaker's job is to arrange good marriages. This scary woman has little patience and very high standards, and she has the power to decide the fate of the young ladies in her village.

The Matchmaker does not approve of Mulan.

She criticised Mulan's manners and her figure, and she thought Mulan talked too much. Things went a little better when Mulan poured the tea, until Cri-Kee took a dip in the cup! Mulan saved the Matchmaker from drinking the cricket, but then set her on fire by mistake! Although Mulan put the fire out, the Matchmaker branded her a "disgrace".

The Matchmaker says Mulan will never bring honour to her family.

Heavy make-up

Job: Arranging good marriages for eligible young girls

Likes: Good manners, being respected, people who are always on time

Dislikes: Young women who speak without permission, clumsiness

Shan-Yu

Shan-Yu is a huge, ferocious Hun. The fearless and brutal warrior will destroy anyone who stands in his way. His falcon acts as a good scout. He is just as vicious and cruel as his master.

Glowing yellow eyes

Shan-Yu's falcon

While Mulan was busy with the Matchmaker, China was facing a much bigger problem. The mighty Great Wall that had been built to protect the country had been breached. Warrior Shan-Yu and his Hun army had scaled the Great Wall and attacked the guards. No one had been able to stop them and now they were marching toward the Imperial City. With Shan-Yu's vicious falcon, leading the way, China was in great danger.

The Imperial guards try to flee as the Huns climb over the Great Wall.

Home: The Hun Empire, north of the Great Wall

Job: Fearsome leader of the Hun army

Goal: To defeat the Emperor and conquer all of China, no matter what it takes!

General Li

General Li has fought in many battles for China, and not lost one yet. He is a strong leader and very smart. His son, Li Shang, is also becoming a great soldier.

General Li informs the Emperor of the attack.

General Li was a high-ranking member of the Chinese Army. When he heard of Shan-Yu's attack, he set off to the Imperial City to warn the Emperor. The General knew that Shan-Yu was dangerous. However, he was confident that his men were strong enough to defeat the Hun invaders. He planned to set up a strong defence around the Imperial Palace to make sure that China's Emperor was protected from any assault.

Travelling cloak

Job: General of the Chinese Army

Likes: Leading his soldiers, serving the Emperor, seeing his son become a Captain

Goal: To stop Shan-Yu's army and protect China

Emperor

The Emperor is famous for his wisdom. He always puts his people's needs first and respects anyone who displays true courage.

The Emperor listened to General Li's plan, but insisted that the troops should be sent to protect his people rather than himself. He ordered his adviser, Chi Fu, to call up all the reserve soldiers. He also told him to search all the provinces of China for as many new recruits as possible. The Emperor wanted to build a bigger, stronger army to make sure that his people would be safe from Shan-Yu and his Hun army. He believed that even one man could be the difference between victory and defeat.

The Emperor orders Chi Fu to recruit more troops.

Flowing, white beard

Home: The Great Palace, Imperial City

Job: Ruler of Imperial China

Strengths: Great wisdom and courage – he is not afraid of Shan-Yu and he will always protect his people

Chi Fu

Chi Fu is proud to carry out the Emperor's orders – perhaps a little too proud. He likes bossing other people around and believes that women should be quiet and obedient.

Chi Fu is committed to his mission.

Chi Fu followed the Emperor's orders precisely. He travelled all around China, ordering one man from each family to join the army. When he reached Mulan's village, he ordered her father, Fa Zhou, to enlist. Despite being ill, Fa Zhou agreed to serve the Emperor. Mulan

Official tablet for notes

was very upset, as she knew that her father was not strong enough to fight. Mulan prayed

Fa Zhou proudly accepts the Emperor's orders.

to her ancestors for strength and then made a brave decision to save her father.

Job: Emperor's Council Member

Likes: Feeling important, being bossy

Dislikes: Putting up with annoying soldiers, silly women who dare to speak in the presence of a man!

Mulan the soldier

Mulan just wants to protect her father. She doesn't really think about how dangerous her plan is, or how hard it will be pretending to be a man all the time.

Mulan prepares to become a brave soldier.

Protective shoulder pads

Short hair tied back

Fa Zhou's armour

Sword of the Ancestor

While her family slept, Mulan stole her father's sword and armour. She used the sword to cut off her hair and then put on the armour. She would pretend to be a man and join the army in her father's place! Her disguise was so good that when Mulan sneaked into the stables, the family horse, Khan, didn't even recognise her. She soon reassured him and they quickly set off to find the army training camp.

Before they reached the camp, Mulan decided she needed to practise being manly. After spending so long trying to be the perfect lady, now she needed to become the perfect man instead. Unfortunately, she found that just as difficult. Her voice was too high, her walk was all wrong – she couldn't even hold her sword properly. She would never be able to convince a whole camp of soldiers that she was one of them. Khan was not much help either – he thought her efforts were really funny!

The army training camp is built for thousands of soldiers.

Khan

Khan is an old war horse. He has taken part in many battles with Mulan's father. But these days he is more likely to be trotting to the village shop and back.

Reins to control Khan

Likes: Riding with Mulan

Dislikes: Being called a cow or a sheep – or any other silly names, for that matter!

Goal: To help Mulan get through the war, and to keep her safe from harm

Ancestors

The Fa Ancestors watch over the current family and are supposed to help them in times of need. However, they are often too busy arguing among themselves to agree on anything.

Mulan's family is heartbroken – they can't bear to have lost her.

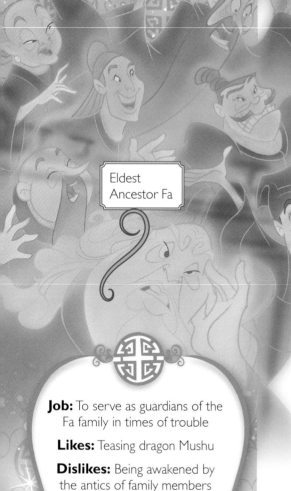

Eldest Ancestor Fa

Job: To serve as guardians of the Fa family in times of trouble

Likes: Teasing dragon Mushu

Dislikes: Being awakened by the antics of family members like Mulan. They always knew she was trouble!

When Mulan's family realised what she had done, they knew that it was too late to stop her. If Fa Zhou went after her and revealed her true identity, Mulan would be killed for treason and the family would be disgraced. So Grandmother Fa prayed to the Ancestors for help, and this time the Ancestors were listening. They decided to watch over Mulan and keep her safe. They chose a powerful stone dragon to go after her.

Mushu, a small red dragon, was sent to wake up the stone dragon, but he accidentally demolished it instead. Unwilling to admit his mistake to the Ancestors, Mushu went after Mulan himself. With Cri-Kee's help, he was determined to ensure that she become a war hero. But first, he needed to help her fit in with the other soldiers. However, thanks to Mushu's advice, Mulan accidentally caused a big brawl in the camp. It was hardly the best way to begin her army training.

Mulan isn't too impressed with Mushu at first.

Mushu

For a tiny dragon, Mushu has a big personality. He is a fast-talking expert on everything. He might only be little, but Mushu has big plans for Mulan.

Gong to awaken Ancestors

Job: Gong ringer – until he can convince the Ancestors to promote him, that is!

Likes: Impressing the Ancestors, helping Mulan, pretending to be much bigger than he actually is

Dislikes: Being called a lizard

Li Shang

Shang is a fine soldier. He is strong, agile and focussed. He is eager to prove that he can be a great military leader, just like his father, General Li.

General Li's son, Captain Li Shang, was in charge of the army training camp and he wasn't impressed with his new recruits, especially the young troublemaker, Mulan. Shang asked Mulan her name. She had to think fast to come up with a boy's name – she chose Ping. Shang warned Ping and the rest of the soldiers that their training would be hard. He would be teaching them how to use discipline and strength to become great warriors. He could see that his men had a lot to learn before they could face Shan-Yu's frightening Hun army.

Strengths: Leadership, great bravery

Likes: Structure and rules, seeing his troops improve under his training

Dislikes: Liars, lazy soldiers, being called a bad Captain

Bright red cape

Training for battle is tough!

At first, Mulan found the training difficult. The other men played tricks on her and

she didn't think she would ever be as strong or skilled as Shang.

The soldiers in the army love playing tricks on young Ping.

Even tough guys like Yao were struggling and Shang began to think that his men would never be ready for war. Tired of Mulan's failure, Shang decided

to send her home, but Mulan refused to give up. She proved to Shang that she did have discipline and strength after all.

Mulan completes a very tricky mission.

She was just as tough as any man and deserved her place in the army!

Yao

Yao is often getting into fights, but he is not a soldier. He is more of a brawler who loves making trouble. He has a quick temper, but he is a loyal friend, too.

Recruit's simple robe

Likes: Being tough, arguing with people, showing off his muscles

Dislikes: Being called names, Mulan getting in his way

Nickname: King of the Rock – a name that he gave to himself!

Chien-Po

This gentle giant is stronger than most of the other people in Li Shang's army. Chien-Po is happy, as long as he has a full stomach and his pals around him.

Mulan had not only proved herself to Shang, but she had also earned her fellow soldiers' respect. Yao and his friends Chien-Po and Ling stopped teasing her, and Shang knew he finally had an army that he could be proud of. However, Chi Fu disagreed, and believed that they still weren't ready to fight. So Mushu and Cri-Kee decided to change his mind by faking a letter from the "General", which said that he needed the recruits' help. Mulan was off to fight her first battle!

Strong, but friendly grip

The General's messenger is really Cri-Kee, in a fake suit, with a little help from Mushu.

Likes: Making new friends, calming people down with his chanting

Dislikes: Swimming, Yao's temper

Favourite food: Beef, pork, chicken…anything tasty, really!

A shocking defeat

Ling

Ling is a skinny joker who wishes he had done more exercise before joining the army. He does not notice that Ping is a girl, despite bathing next to "him"!

Clueless expression

However, when the soldiers reached the battlefield, they saw that General Li had been defeated. Shang and his recruits were the Emperor's last hope so they set off to the Imperial City. Unfortunately, an accidental explosion caused by Mushu revealed their whereabouts to Shan-Yu. Outnumbered by the Huns, the battle looked hopeless. But then a quick-thinking Mulan created an avalanche. It buried the Huns in snow, but almost cost Mulan and Shang their lives.

Getting rid of the large Hun army will take a clever plan.

Likes: Joking around, causing mischief, pretty girls

Dislikes: Snakes, too much exercise, going on long marches

Favourite prank: Putting a beetle down Ping's shirt!

Ready for action

Mulan's determination has turned her from a girl in disguise to a true soldier. She is more than a match for any man. Why should it matter that she's a girl?

Loose-fitting robe

Dark green sash

Flat, practical shoes

Mulan had defeated Shan-Yu, but she was injured. When the doctor treated her wounds, her true identity was revealed. Shang was angry, but he sent her away instead of killing her. Mulan planned to return home in disgrace, while the soldiers marched on to the Imperial City. However, she learned that Shan-Yu had actually survived, and rushed to warn Shang. At first he wouldn't listen to her, but then Shan-Yu captured the Emperor, and only Mulan had a plan to save him.

The Emperor is in trouble. Can Mulan come up with the perfect rescue plan in time?

Mulan, Yao, Chien Po, Ling and Shang climbed the palace walls. While Shang saved the Emperor, Mulan once again defeated Shan-Yu, with a little help from Mushu. Instead of punishing Mulan for her "lie", the Emperor thanked her for saving everyone. He offered her Chi Fu's job, but Mulan just wanted to go home. With the Emperor's help, Shang finally realised that Mulan was not just a great soldier, she was also a special woman.

Mulan makes a daring escape from the roof of the palace.

Mulan and Shang's friendship blossoms into romance.

A special girl

Mulan is happy to be home. She has found a way to bring honour to the Fa family, while being true to herself. She might even have found a good husband, too.

Comfortable, stylish robe

Strong colours

Elegant hairstyle

Diamond necklace

Long, silky gloves

The Princess and the Frog

New Orleans was filled with music and fun times, but Tiana's days were filled with nothing but hard work. It would take a whirlwind adventure and some wonderful new friends to help her realise what was really important in life.

Contents

Little Tiana

Even as a child, Tiana is serious about her ambitions. Unlike her friend Charlotte, she is not prepared to kiss a frog to get what she wants. In fact, Tiana is scared of the slimy creatures!

Tiana and Charlotte love listening to fairy tales.

Tiny bunch

Likes: Listening to stories with her friend Charlotte, creating new recipes with her father, getting people to try her tasty food

Favourite colour: Green

New Orleans was a beautiful city on the Mississippi River, famous for its food and its jazz music. It was also home to two little girls, Tiana and Charlotte. Although they were best friends, the two girls had very different lives. Tiana shared a small, cosy house with her hard-working parents. Charlotte lived in a huge mansion with her rich, doting father. The girls' personalities were very different, too. Tiana was a practical person and her ambition was to open her own restaurant when she was older. Charlotte was a dreamer and her greatest wish was to become a princess.

Even as a little girl, Tiana had a great talent for cooking. She loved to create delicious dishes and share them with her family and neighbours. Her best friend, Charlotte, might have had all the pretty dresses she could ever wish for, but Tiana wasn't jealous – she was

Charlotte will even kiss a real, icky frog to find her prince!

happy. Tiana's little home was always filled with love, kindness and great cooking smells. So, while fairy-tale-loving Charlotte was ready to kiss a hundred frogs in order to become a real princess, sensible Tiana planned to achieve her goals through hard work instead.

Little Charlotte

Charlotte is used to getting what she wants, thanks to her rich father. She believes in fairy tales and often wishes on the Evening Star. But she doesn't like waiting for her wishes to come true.

Curly blonde hair

Princess-like dress

Likes: Fairy tales, playing with her fluffy pets, presents, wishing on stars, dreaming of finding her true love

Favourite outfit: Anything that makes her look like a pretty princess!

Eudora

Eudora is proud of her hard-working husband and clever daughter. They might not be a rich family, but they are a happy one. That is more than enough for Eudora.

Kind expression

Tiana's mother, Eudora, was the finest seamstress in New Orleans. Her talented fingers were responsible for creating Charlotte's fabulous, fit-for-a-princess wardrobe. Charlotte was her best customer! Eudora often read fairy tales to Charlotte and Tiana while she worked. Eudora

Charlotte loves her beautiful princess dresses.

believed in working hard to get what she wanted, but she couldn't help thinking there was more to life than work. Eudora thought love and happiness were much more important.

Eudora is a really good storyteller.

Job: The finest seamstress in New Orleans

Likes: Making dresses, spending time with her family, telling stories

Dislikes: Tiana working too hard

An extra touch of spice always makes the gumbo special.

James

James believes in working hard and he wants his daughter to be just like him. He knows that she can't just wish for something to happen. Tiana must make her dreams come true for herself.

Tiana inherited her talent for cooking from her father, James. He believed that good food could bring different people together and make them happy. James taught Tiana how to make his specialty dish – a thick soup known as gumbo. He told her about his dream of owning a restaurant. He had found an old sugar mill that would be perfect. He also came up with the perfect name – Tiana's Place. When James passed away, Tiana was determined to make her father's dream come true.

Brown braces

Likes: Cooking with Tiana, sharing food with his neighbours

Favourite food: Gumbo

Beliefs: You must never forget what is important – family, friendship and love.

A busy girl

Tiana wants to make her father's dream a reality, so she can't think of anything except work. There is no room for fun. She has never even learned how to dance!

When she grew up, Tiana worked hard to earn enough money to open a restaurant.

Tiana saves all her money for her dream restaurant.

She had two jobs – at night she waited on tables at Cal's Diner and during the day she served coffee and made deep-fried pastries called beignets at Duke's Cafe. She had no time to go dancing with her friends and she was always tired, but Tiana didn't mind. By saving up her wages and tips, she nearly had enough money to buy the sugar mill.

Hot, fresh beignets

Job: Waitress

Dream: To open her own restaurant, called Tiana's Place

Likes: Cooking, earning her own money

Dislikes: Lazy people

Customers love cheerful Tiana and always give her generous tips.

Tiana makes the best
sugar-dusted beignets!

Eli "Big Daddy" LaBouff

Eli LaBouff is a powerful businessman. But one person can always make him do what she wants – Charlotte. Big Daddy is a complete pushover when it comes to his daughter.

Curly moustache

Charlotte's father, Eli "Big Daddy" LaBouff, was one of Tiana's best customers. He couldn't get enough of her tasty beignets, and he was rich enough to afford as many as he could eat. In fact, Big Daddy was one of the wealthiest men in New Orleans – being a successful sugar baron made life very sweet. He adored his daughter, Charlotte, and had just been chosen as king of the Mardi Gras festival for the fifth year in a row.

Job: Sugar baron

Likes: Making Charlotte happy, eating Tiana's delicious food

Dislikes: Charlotte talking over him – she never lets him finish a sentence!

Grown-up Charlotte

Charlotte is so focussed on becoming a princess that she forgets to think about others. She doesn't even notice that Tiana is finally buying a restaurant.

Stylish up-do with a tiara

Likes: Romance, dancing, pretty dresses, gossiping

Dislikes: Having to wait for what she wants

Dream: To marry a handsome prince and become a princess

Charlotte was all grown up, but her dreams hadn't changed – she still wanted to be a princess. When she learned that a prince was visiting New Orleans, Charlotte was not about to let him get away. Of course, her doting daddy fixed everything and invited the prince to a masquerade ball at his mansion. Charlotte was sure that he would fall in love with her. However, just to make sure, she asked her friend Tiana to make some of her tasty beignets and bring them to the ball.

Charlotte wants to buy Tiana's yummy beignets for the ball.

Tiana knows the old sugar mill will make a perfect restaurant.

Fenner brothers

Henry and Harvey Fenner are brothers and New Orleans' premier estate agents. They make huge profits by selling properties to the highest bidders.

Fancy top hat

Charlotte paid a lot of money for the beignets. This meant that Tiana finally had enough money for the down payment on her restaurant. She met with the estate agents, the Fenner brothers, and arranged to sign the contracts for the sugar mill at the ball. Tiana was overjoyed. All her hard work had been worth it. Her mother was so proud of her, and she knew that her daddy would have been, too.

Tiana can always rely on Eudora for support.

Job: Estate agents

Likes: Making deals, selling properties

Dislikes: Having to wait for their money – the quicker they can get their hands on cash, the better

Prince Naveen

Fun-loving and free-spirited Prince Naveen doesn't take life too seriously. He has never had to do anything for himself – that's what his servants are for!

Handsome Prince Naveen is confident that he can make any girl fall in love with him.

The people of New Orleans were excited by the arrival of Prince Naveen of Maldonia. What they didn't know was the real reason behind his visit. Naveen loved jazz music, dancing and beautiful women – but he did not love working! His parents had grown tired of his laid-back attitude and cut off his allowance. He did not want to get a job, so he had come to New Orleans to find a rich wife!

Ukulele to make foot-tapping music

Home: Polished-marble palace in Maldonia

Likes: Jazz music, dancing, travelling, serenading lovely women

Dislikes: Hard work, responsibility

Lawrence

Lawrence would love to be the one giving the orders, rather than carrying them out. He is desperate for some respect, and will go to any lengths to get it…even if it means getting involved in some bad magic.

The prince's downtrodden valet, Lawrence, was supposed to take care of the prince. His job was to make him look elegant, act regally and behave respectably. It wasn't easy! Lawrence always seemed to be left carrying the prince's bags or trying to get him out of trouble. Meanwhile the prince just laughed and carried on having fun. Lawrence was sick and tired of not getting any reward for his hard work. He wanted things to change!

Spotless coat

Lawrence hates Naveen's carefree attitude to life.

Job: Royal valet

Home: Wherever Prince Naveen goes. Lawrence doesn't have a choice!

Dislikes: Being bossed around by Prince Naveen

Dr Facilier

Dr Facilier will use anyone or anything to help him become rich and powerful. However, bad magic is very dangerous. Dr Facilier might just find himself in big trouble if his plan fails.

Skull and crossbones

Magical tarot card

Lurking nearby was a wicked fortune teller called Dr Facilier. He was very jealous of Big Daddy and Charlotte's money and wanted it for himself. When Prince Naveen and Lawrence arrived, Dr Facilier saw the perfect opportunity to get his bony hands on the LaBouff fortune. He offered to read the trusting prince's tarot cards, but instead he turned Naveen into a frog. He then gave Lawrence a magical locket that transformed him into the prince.

Dr Facilier uses bad magic to trap Naveen.

Job: Telling fortunes and granting wishes – for a price

Goal: To gain the LaBouff family's fortune and rule New Orleans

Abilities: Bad magic

Likes: Money and power

Lawrence attends the ball, disguised as Prince Naveen.

Ready for the ball

Tiana has always believed that hard work will bring her what she wants. She is not so sure any more. She has come so close to getting her restaurant, but it seems further away than ever before. What will she do now?

Tiara for perfect princess look

Sparkly silver necklace

Long blue gloves

That night, at the masquerade ball, Charlotte was thrilled when her prince finally arrived and asked her for a romantic dance. Tiana was happy for her friend, but her own night was about to be ruined. The Fenner brothers had received a higher offer for the sugar mill. Tiana's restaurant dream was over unless she could find more money! She was heartbroken and accidentally ruined her dress, so Charlotte lent her one of her own ball gowns. Tiana looked like a princess, but she was too upset to care.

Tiana wishes upon the Evening Star for her dream to come true.

The frog prince

Naveen is not happy about being transformed into a tiny, slimy frog. He keeps tripping over his huge feet, and he does not enjoy being chased by hungry alligators.

An unexpected guest arrives at the party.

Charming grin

Striped legs

Charlotte believed that wishing on the Evening Star could make your dreams come true, so a desperate Tiana decided to try it – and a frog appeared! Tiana couldn't believe her eyes, and when she jokingly offered to kiss it, she couldn't believe her ears either – it answered her! Tiana's first instinct was to squash the slimy creature, but then she decided to listen to him. He told her that he was Prince Naveen and that a kiss from a "princess" like her might break the spell he was under.

Tiana grabs a book to squash the talking frog. Good thing he can jump!

Tiana hates the idea of kissing a frog, but does it anyway. She will do anything to get her restaurant.

Tiana transformed

Tiana thought her day could not get any worse. But she is wrong. She turns into a slimy frog and is also stuck with the frog Prince Naveen. She can't stand the wise-cracking big mouth!

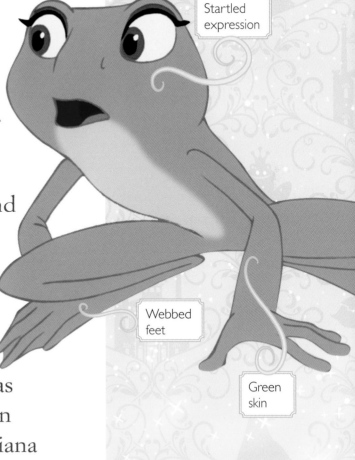

Startled expression

Webbed feet

Green skin

Reluctantly, Tiana agreed to kiss the prince in exchange for the money to buy her restaurant. Unfortunately, the plan backfired and Tiana became a frog as well. Finding themselves to be unwelcome guests at the masquerade ball, Naveen and Tiana escaped on a balloon. As they drifted toward the swampy bayou, the froggy pair got to know each other. They weren't impressed – Tiana thought the prince was spoiled and lazy, and Naveen was upset to find out that Tiana wasn't a real princess.

Louis

This gentle giant from the swamps of Louisiana loves his trumpet, Giselle. He dreams of playing in a real jazz band. He did try once. But the musicians got scared and tried to shoot him!

Louis just needs someone to jam with, and Naveen is the perfect companion!

Jazz trumpet

Pointy teeth and goofy grin

Dream: To be a great jazz musician

Likes: Good food, playing jazz classics on his trumpet,

Dislikes: Mean hunters, accidentally scaring people

Tiana was determined to get back to New Orleans and fix their problems, so she built a raft. While the resourceful waitress paddled the raft, the pampered prince lay back strumming on a homemade ukulele. Suddenly, a huge alligator appeared! Instead of trying to eat the tasty frogs, he started playing music with Naveen. His name was Louis and he eventually agreed to lead them to someone who might be able to help break the spell.

During their journey through the bayou, Tiana and Naveen met a friendly firefly named Ray. He pointed out that Louis was taking them in the wrong direction. Ray offered to show them the right way, with a little help from his firefly family. Along the way, Tiana and Naveen faced many dangers, from hungry frog hunters to spooky shadows sent by Dr Facilier. As they learned to work together, Tiana and Naveen realised that maybe they had been wrong about each other…

Ray

Romantic Ray is a firefly with a big heart. He is madly in love with Evangeline. But Evangeline is not a firefly – she is the Evening Star. Ray does not know that. He just thinks she is just a little shy and quiet.

Brightly lit tail

Naveen teaches Tiana how to dance.

Dream: To be with his beloved Evangeline – the Evening Star

Likes: Romance, helping people, his firefly family

Abilities: He can zap any troublemakers with lightning from his tail!

Mama Odie

She might be 197 years old, toothless and blind, but Mama Odie is also wise and powerful. Her pet snake, Juju, helps her with her spells, and keeps her from falling into her own gumbo pot.

Seeing-eye snake, Juju

Mama Odie lives in a boat in a tree.

Job: Queen of the Bayou

Likes: Gumbo, using her magic and potions to help people get what they truly need

Best friend: Her pet snake, Juju

Finally, Tiana and Naveen reached a strange old lady named Mama Odie. She told them to work out the difference between what they wanted, and what they needed. She said that a kiss from Charlotte, the Mardi Gras princess, before midnight, would break the spell cast on Naveen. But Naveen didn't want to kiss Charlotte – he was in love with Tiana. However, he knew that if he didn't kiss Charlotte, Tiana would never get her restaurant, so he didn't reveal how he felt.

As they arrived back in New Orleans, Naveen was captured by Dr Facilier, but Tiana had no idea. Soon after, she saw Charlotte marry "Prince Naveen". She thought the spell had been broken, but it was Lawrence in disguise. Clever Ray saw what had happened. He stole Lawrence's magic locket and gave it to Tiana. Dr Facilier was desperate to get the locket back, so he offered Tiana her restaurant in exchange for the locket. Tiana refused and smashed the locket, making it lose all its power. Lawrence looked like himself again and Dr Facilier was destroyed.

Tempting deal

Dr Facilier shows Tiana a vision of what she could have if she makes a deal with him. She sees herself as a human again, and the owner of an elegant restaurant. It's everything she dreamed it would be – but now she has a new dream.

Magic locket

Pearl necklace

Tiana smashes the magic locket.

Tiana in love

Tiana finally understands what Mama Odie had said. She now knows the difference between what she wants and what she needs. Tiana might want a restaurant, but she needs Naveen.

Crown of lilies

Lily blossoms for the dress

Beautiful green lily pads

Naveen explained the whole situation to Charlotte and offered to marry her if she would break the spell and help Tiana buy her restaurant. However, Tiana couldn't let that happen. She told Naveen that she loved him and he confessed that he loved her, too. Charlotte recognised true love when she saw it and offered to kiss Naveen, without getting anything in return. Unfortunately, Charlotte's kiss didn't work and Naveen and Tiana remained frogs. They decided to go back to the bayou and asked Mama Odie to marry them. As they kissed, Tiana and Naveen became human again.

So what if they are frogs? At least they have true love!

Tiana had become a princess when she married Naveen, so she was able to break the spell. The happy couple returned to New Orleans and had a royal wedding, in front of all of their friends and family. After all the celebrations, Tiana and Naveen got to work on fixing up the old sugar mill. Before long, Princess Tiana opened her own restaurant, but with a brand new name – Tiana's Palace! With Tiana's wonderful cooking and Naveen's jazzy music, the restaurant was a huge hit. People came from all walks of life to taste Tiana's delicious food, just as her father had promised.

A dream come true

Tiana is sure that her daddy would have been proud of her. She finally owns a restaurant, but has also learned what is truly important – love.

Royal crown

Fashionable dress

Tiana's Palace has a grand opening night.

Bodice with
pink ribbon

Homemade
dress

Hair is 21
metres long

Tangled

High up in a tower, a young
girl with long hair was hidden from the
outside world. When a runaway thief tried
to use Rapunzel's home as a hideout, she
would finally discover all that life
had to offer, and the truth about
who she really was.

Contents

Mother Gothel

Mother Gothel is obsessed with her looks and will do anything to avoid growing old. She only cares about how she looks on the outside. But inside, at heart, she is mean and crafty.

Long, flowing, red gown

When a drop of sunlight fell to Earth, it created a magical flower. This golden bloom had the power to heal people and keep them young if they sang a special song to it. An old woman named Mother Gothel found the flower, but she was very selfish. She chose to use its magic to remain young forever. For hundreds of years, Gothel guarded the flower, to make sure that no one else ever discovered it.

A special song awakens the flower's magic, and its petals glow golden.

Dream: To always be young and beautiful

Likes: Rapunzel's hair, looking at herself in the mirror, being totally wrinkle-free

Dislikes: Being disobeyed, getting older

Gothel lived on the edge of a bustling kingdom, ruled by a wise King and a kind Queen. The Queen was expecting a baby. Sadly, she fell ill and only the magical golden flower could save her. Her servants searched everywhere and finally found it. Sure enough, it healed the Queen. She gave birth to a healthy, golden-haired baby girl named Rapunzel. To celebrate the princess's birth, the King and Queen released a glowing, floating lantern.

King and Queen

The King and Queen are popular rulers and loving parents. They are so proud of their precious baby daughter. They can't wait to teach her how to be a princess. After all, one day, Rapunzel will rule the kingdom.

Royal jewels

The lantern floats high up into the sky.

Job: King and Queen of the kingdom

Home: A beautiful castle

Likes: Their loyal subjects, playing with their daughter, throwing parties

Rapunzel

After spending almost eighteen years in a tower, Rapunzel has grown – and so has her hair! She may not have seen much of the world, but this curious girl longs for an adventure!

Really long, silky, golden hair

Without the flower, Mother Gothel needed a new way to stay young. She discovered that the flower's magic had been transferred into Rapunzel's hair. Gothel kidnapped Rapunzel and hid her in a tower in the middle of a forest. She raised Rapunzel as her own daughter and told the trusting young girl scary stories about the world outside the tower. She needed to make sure Rapunzel was too afraid to ever want to leave!

Mother Gothel climbs Rapunzel's long hair to get into the tower.

Dream: To see the floating lights on her birthday

Likes: Painting, reading, dancing…anything to pass the time!

Secret Weapon: A frying pan – she can knock out any intruder with it!

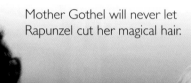

Mother Gothel will never let Rapunzel cut her magical hair.

Rapunzel loves painting the walls of her tower.

Pascal

Silent Pascal looks out for Rapunzel and follows her everywhere. He perches patiently on her shoulder or her head. Pascal wants Rapunzel to play with him outside the tower. But she just won't leave!

Rapunzel tried to fill her days with as many fun activities as possible. Her only friend, a chameleon named Pascal, kept her company. But the older she got, the more she longed to see the world outside her tower. She dreamed about the floating lanterns that filled the sky every year on her birthday. One day, Rapunzel found the courage to ask Gothel if she could take a trip. She wanted to see the floating lanterns for herself. Evil Gothel said no – she planned to keep Rapunzel and her magical hair all to herself.

Big beady eyes

Forest-green scales

Likes: Helping Rapunzel, playing hide and seek

Dislikes: Being called a frog, being bored, strangers

Abilities: Can change colour to blend into his surroundings, no matter where he is

Flynn Rider

Flynn Rider likes to think of himself as a smooth-talking outlaw. But at heart, he is a kind orphan named Eugene Fitzherbert. He will do anything for someone he loves.

Rapunzel felt trapped in her tower, but to the charming criminal, Flynn Rider, it looked like the perfect place to hide. Flynn had stolen a precious crown from the royal palace with two scary thieves, known as the Stabbington brothers. But while they were making their escape, he decided to ditch the brothers and keep the crown for himself. Now, he was on the run with a stolen crown, and two angry thugs and a troop of royal guards chasing behind him. Flynn had been in some scrapes before, but this was definitely his worst.

The Stabbington brothers want to get rid of Flynn, but he tricks them and escapes.

Satchel holds stolen crown

Vain Flynn hates how his nose looks in his Wanted poster!

Dream: To have his own castle

Dislikes: Wanted posters – they never get his good looks right!

Favourite book: *The Tales of Flynnigan Rider* that inspired him to change his name

When Flynn found Rapunzel's tower, he quickly climbed up. All he wanted was a place to lay low until his enemies stopped looking for him. But Rapunzel wasn't taking any chances – she whacked him with a frying pan! Instead of telling Gothel about him, Rapunzel hid him in her wardrobe and asked Gothel to run an errand so that she would leave the tower for a few days. With Gothel gone, Rapunzel tied Flynn up with her hair and offered him a deal. She would return the crown to him, if he would take her to see the floating lanterns.

Stabbington brothers

The Stabbington brothers are mean, vicious brutes, and can't stand being fooled. They plan to make Flynn Rider sorry that he ever met them.

Leather Jacket

For once, Flynn can't charm his way out of a scrape.

Job: They don't have one – they would rather steal money than work for it.

Likes: Treasure, dirty schemes, getting revenge

Dislikes: Flynn Rider, being chased by guards

Hook Hand

Hook Hand understands Rapunzel's need to follow her dreams. He has always wanted to be a concert pianist. However, he doesn't think so highly of Flynn's selfish dream to be rich!

Rapunzel is about to step on grass for the very first time!

Sharp and scary hook

Dream: To be a famous concert pianist and perform on his very own stage

Favorite composer: Mozart

Likes: Playing the piano, singing a jolly song, helping people follow their dreams

Flynn agreed to Rapunzel's plan, but he secretly hoped to convince her to forget about the lanterns and return to the tower. At first, Rapunzel was tempted to go back – the world outside was wonderful, but scary, and she hated lying to Gothel.

However, Rapunzel felt free for the first time in her life and she couldn't bear to give that up just yet. So, Flynn decided to show her just how scary the outside world could be, with a visit to the Snuggly Duckling pub.

Rapunzel keeps her trusty frying pan close.

Big Nose

Big Nose wants to fall in love. He knows he's not the best looking – or best smelling – guy, but he hopes to find someone who can love him. Big Nose insists that deep inside, he's really a lover, not a fighter!

The men in the pub, including Hook Hand and Big Nose, looked like terrifying thugs. But as Rapunzel got to know them, she learned that each one had a dream, just like her. When the royal guards arrived, the men helped their new friend Rapunzel to escape. However, Gothel had also tracked Rapunzel down, and she had a wicked plan to make her return to the tower for good.

Scarred face

Rapunzel charms the band of scary thugs.

Dream: To find a caring woman who will love him despite his scars, bad skin, giant nose…and all his other flaws!

Likes: Romance, rowing boats, giving flowers to pretty girls

Captain of the royal guards

The Captain has built up quite a reputation as the finest guard in the regiment. He prides himself on always catching his man. He won't let Flynn Rider make him look like a fool!

Tough metal helmet

Likes: Law and order, chasing and catching criminals

Dislikes: Escaped prisoners, being tricked

Greatest ally: Maximus, his trusty steed, who has never failed him yet!

The Captain of the royal guards had already captured the Stabbington brothers, but catching Flynn Rider was proving to be a bigger problem. First he had lost Flynn on the way to the tower, and now Flynn had managed to sneak out of the Snuggly Duckling. Luckily, the Captain's loyal horse, Maximus,

The Captain and his horse both hate to lose a chase!

was hot on the ruffian's trail, and they followed Flynn and Rapunzel to a dam. While trying to catch them, Maximus broke the dam, causing a huge flood of water to come crashing down. Rapunzel and Flynn tried to escape by running into a cave, but it seemed to be a dead end. They were trapped!

Rapunzel's magical hair glows underwater.

Rapunzel used her glowing hair to light their way out of the cave, and to heal Flynn's injured hand. Finally, Flynn understood that Rapunzel's hair was magic. He did his best not to look too shocked! As Flynn and Rapunzel began to grow closer, Maximus finally tracked Flynn down and tried to capture him. However, lovely Rapunzel sweet-talked Max into letting Flynn go. She was so

Rapunzel manages to charm Maximus into letting Flynn go…for now.

close to seeing the lanterns now and nothing was going to stand in her way.

Maximus

Maximus is a fast, strong horse, who is also an expert tracker. He is a good judge of character. He adores Rapunzel instantly, but it takes Flynn a little longer to charm him.

Expert nose, for sniffing out criminals

Favourite food: Fresh, crunchy apples

Likes: Leading the other horses, chasing Flynn

Dislikes: Being outsmarted, letting pesky criminals get away

Four little girls

These four little girls love plaiting each other's hair and trying new hairstyles. They can't believe how long and shiny Rapunzel's hair is, and know that it needs their best ever creation.

Rapunzel can't believe she has made it to the kingdom!

Plaiting experts

Hobbies: Creating beautiful hairstyles – the more hair they have to work with, the better!

Likes: Plaiting hair, flowers, skipping, playing by the town fountain, cute animals (like Pascal!)

Finally, Rapunzel arrived in the kingdom. It was even more wonderful than she dreamed it would be! However, as Rapunzel walked among the crowds, her long hair kept on getting in the way. Luckily Flynn found a solution – four little girls with a passion for plaiting. Pretty soon Rapunzel had a new look, and she was free to have fun

The girls do a beautiful job of plaiting.

and explore the town. Somehow, it all seemed strangely familiar, especially the story she heard about a lost princess.

Before long, it was time for the lanterns to be released. Flynn understood how important this day was for Rapunzel. He found the perfect spot for them to watch the stunning display. Rapunzel and Flynn were dazzled by the amazing view. It helped them to realise that they were seeing each other in a new light, too.

The pair are surrounded by glowing lanterns.

Unfortunately, Gothel arrived to ruin the romantic moment, with a little help from the Stabbingtons. The brothers kidnapped Flynn but Gothel told Rapunzel that he had abandoned her. Rapunzel was so upset that she agreed to return home. She believed that Gothel had been right about the world outside the tower after all.

Time to explore

At last, Rapunzel is free to see and do whatever she wants. She is so happy that she sings and dances with joy. Finally, it seems like her life has truly begun.

Flowers decorate plait

Old Gothel

Gothel will do whatever it takes to keep Rapunzel's hair safe. She knows that if it gets cut, it will lose all of its magic powers. She would instantly turn into the old, haggard woman she really is.

Face looks very old

Back in the tower, Rapunzel realised why everything in the kingdom felt so familiar – she was the lost princess! Gothel had been lying to her all along. But Gothel wasn't about to let Rapunzel and her magical hair escape again!

Rapunzel does not want Gothel to touch her magical hair ever again.

Meanwhile, Flynn had been captured by the royal guards. Being in prison gave him time to think, and he realised something, too – he was in love with Rapunzel. Luckily, Maximus fetched the pub thugs to help break Flynn out of jail. Once he was free, he set off to rescue Rapunzel.

When Flynn reached the tower, Gothel wounded him with a blade. Rapunzel tried to heal Flynn, but instead he cut off her hair so she could be free from Gothel. Believing that she could no longer save Flynn without her hair, she cried as she sang her special song. A tear fell onto his face and healed him! At last, Rapunzel could return home to her real parents.

Flynn cuts Rapunzel's hair with some broken glass so that it will lose its power.

Best of all, she had someone special she wanted them to meet.

Princess Rapunzel

Rapunzel always believed that only her hair was magic. Now she knows that the magic is inside her. She plans to share her gift with as many people as possible. Gothel is gone forever!

Natural brown hair

Hair roughly cut short

Rapunzel is home at last.

Arrows always kept sharp

Well-loved bow

Leather belt

Brave

Princess Merida had always had a
wild spirit – she preferred a well-shot arrow
to a well-mannered suitor. Her strong will
and wish for freedom brought chaos to her
kingdom and her family. It would take
all of her bravery to make things
right and change her fate.

Contents

Little Merida

Young Merida is a free-spirited, adventurous child. She loves to explore the wild, but beautiful, countryside around her home, DunBroch Castle. The wee redheaded princess may be small, but she is very brave.

With her father's training, Merida is sure to be an expert archer.

Bright red, unruly hair

Many years ago, a princess named Merida lived in the Highlands of Scotland. The Highlands were an enchanting place to grow up, with their green valleys and shimmering lochs. Merida spent many happy days playing games with her mother, while her father taught her how to shoot a bow and arrow. There were always new places to explore. One day Merida even found mysterious creatures called Will O' the Wisps. Her mother told her that following wisps could lead you to your fate.

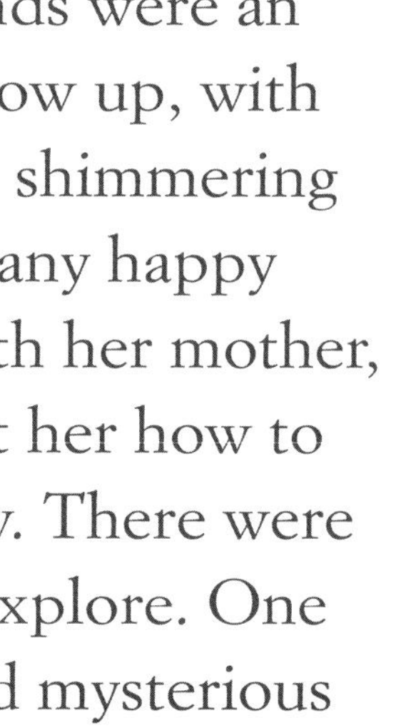

Merida can't believe that the magical wisps are real

Home: A great castle in the Kingdom of DunBroch

Likes: Shooting arrows, playing in the forest, spending time with her parents

Favourite game: Hide and seek

Merida's mother, Queen Elinor, ruled the kingdom with her husband, King Fergus. She was a wise queen, and worked hard to keep peace between the different clans in the Highlands. Elinor loved her fearless daughter, but she wished that Merida would behave more like a traditional princess. Elinor knew that being a princess was a great responsibility. She tried hard to prepare Merida by passing on her wisdom. Elinor believed that it was Merida's duty to do what was right for her kingdom, not just for herself.

When Merida is afraid of a storm, Elinor sings her a gentle lullaby.

Queen Elinor

The elegant Queen Elinor is a strong and wise leader of her kingdom. Although she rarely raises her voice, one stern look from her can make a tough clansman tremble in his kilt.

Jewelled, gold tiara

Job: Queen of DunBroch

Likes: Following tradition, fulfilling her duties as queen, sewing beautiful tapestries

Dislikes: Princesses having weapons – especially when they leave them on the dinner table!

King Fergus

King Fergus is so proud of Merida. He thinks she is tough, brave and strong – just like him. He loves his wife and children, and always does his best to make sure they are all happy.

While Queen Elinor ruled with grace and patience, King Fergus was fierce and loud. However, his kind heart and good sense of humour meant that his people loved him. Stories of his bravery were legendary. Many years ago, he had united the clans and led them to victory against invaders from the sea. This was why the clan leaders had chosen him as their king. Fergus would do anything to protect his kingdom and his family. Once, he even lost a leg while saving his wife and daughter from a huge bear named Mor'du. Ever since, he had been obsessed with hunting bears.

Fergus loves playing with his young triplet princes.

Title: The Bear King

Goal: To defeat Mor'du and avenge the loss of his leg

Likes: Telling stories of his best battles, joking around with Merida, playing with his dogs

Wooden peg leg

Merida dares to climb the scary Crone's Tooth. Only the bravest kings had done this before.

Merida

Merida wishes Queen Elinor would try to understand how she feels. She hates having to spend all of her time learning how to be as perfect as her mother. All she wants to do is be herself.

As the years passed, Merida grew into a strong-willed young woman. She didn't like to be told what to do, what to wear or

how to behave. Unfortunately, her mother had other ideas. Elinor thought that it was time Merida found a

Elinor cannot tame her daugher's wild hair or her free spirit.

husband, one who would help to unite the kingdom. Merida thought she was far too young to get married and she wanted to be free to fall in love whenever – and with whomever – she liked.

Trusty bow

Favourite weapon: Bow and arrow – she never misses a target!

Dislikes: Her duties as a princess, being nagged by the queen

Greatest fear: Losing her freedom

Angus

Angus is always happy to go galloping across the glens with Merida whenever she wants a break from her royal duties. Angus loves exploring, but is terrified of anything magical.

Sometimes it seemed to Merida that the only one who really listened to her was her horse, Angus. Going riding with him helped her forget all about her troubles. Her mother, however, had decided that Merida's days of riding and exploring were over. She invited the three lords of the kingdom – and their eldest sons – to DunBroch Castle. The sons would compete in the Highland Games and the prize would be Merida's hand in marriage!

Angus has always been Merida's best friend and loyal companion.

Silky, black mane

Best friend: Merida

Likes: Exploring with Merida, riding through the forest

Dislikes: Will O' the Wisps and other magical beings

Favourite food: Oats

The three clans sail across the loch.

The lords arrived at DunBroch Castle, each one eager for his son to succeed. Like Merida, the suitors were not too happy with the idea of marriage. However, they didn't dare disobey their fathers. Thankfully, Merida was much bolder than them, and she had secretly come up with a plan. According to Scottish law, the first born of each of the great leaders could enter the Games. Merida realised that since she was the first born

Young MacGuffin seems like a nervous lad. Will he be able to hit the bulls-eye?

of DunBroch, that included her, too! As the princess, she could choose the contest. She chose archery, knowing she would be able to win. Young MacGuffin was the first to shoot.

MacGuffins

The big and brawny MacGuffins are famous for their size and strength. Lord MacGuffin claims that his son once defeated 2,000 foes with his bare hands. Young MacGuffin, however, is gentle and hates fighting.

Thick beard

Sturdy boots

Clan symbol: A cauldron

Likes: Lord MacGuffin loves battle, but his son wants to make friends – if only someone could understand what he is saying!

Abilities: Both MacGuffins are very tough and strong.

Macintoshes

Lord Macintosh prides himself on leading a clan of fierce warriors. However, Young Macintosh is more fragile than fierce. He has a habit of bursting into tears when things don't go his way.

Blue war paint

Clan symbol: A lyre

Likes: Both Macintoshes are proud of their long black hair. Young Macintosh likes to impress ladies by flexing his muscles

Dislikes: Being insulted

Red tartan

The clansfolk watched as Young MacGuffin's shot barely hit the target. Merida and Fergus thought his efforts were extremely funny and joked that he was probably better at holding up bridges than archery! Next up was the vain Young Macintosh. When he missed the bullseye, he lost his temper. He started screaming and he threw his bow away into the crowd! Merida and Fergus were less than impressed with his childish reaction, and they couldn't help making fun of his silly behaviour. Elinor wished that Merida and Fergus would both take the contest seriously – the future of the kingdom was at stake!

Young Macintosh throws a tantrum when he cannot hit the target.

Merida's final suitor was Wee Dingwall. At first Merida felt sorry for the scrawny boy, who looked like he could barely lift his bow. However, when he miraculously hit the bullseye, she was seriously worried that she might have to marry him. It was time to put her plan into action. Announcing herself as the competitor from clan DunBroch, Merida took aim for her own hand in marriage – and hit all three bullseyes! Merida was proud of herself, but her mother was furious.

Everyone is shocked when Merida wins the contest.

Dingwalls

Lord Dingwall is a hot-tempered Highlander and he prefers fighting to talking. His son is a lot calmer. However, when Lord Dingwall needs his son's help, Wee Dingwall is a surprisingly scrappy fighter!

Long moustache

Scrawny body

Clan symbol: A rock

Dislikes: Lord Dingwall hates being short, so he often stands on a stool

Talents: Wee Dingwall may look harmless, but he uses his sharp teeth to bite his opponents.

Reluctant Princess

Merida's mother forces her to wear a tight and uncomfortable outfit during the Games. When Merida competes in the archery contest, she ends up ripping her dress and letting her unruly hair fly free.

Elinor couldn't believe how her daughter had behaved. She was hurt and embarrassed, and worried that Merida's actions would lead to war between the clans. But Merida couldn't believe Elinor still wasn't listening to her about not getting married. Mother and daughter got angrier and angrier, until Merida slashed her mother's special tapestry and Elinor threw Merida's bow into the fire. Elinor regretted her actions, but Merida was so upset that she galloped away with Angus.

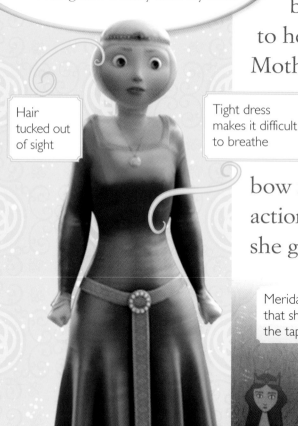

Hair tucked out of sight

Tight dress makes it difficult to breathe

Delicate embroidery

Merida doesn't care that she ruined the tapestry.

Merida remembers what her mother told her about wisps. She knows she must follow them.

Merida rode until she reached an ancient stone circle. There, she met some Will O' the Wisps, who led her to a mysterious cottage. Merida found the old woman who lived there was a witch. Merida thought that this could be her chance to solve all her problems. She begged the Witch for a spell that would change her mother. The Witch agreed and gave Merida a magical cake. She told her that if her mother ate it, Merida's fate would be changed forever.

Witch

The Witch looks like an ordinary old woman. However, her talking crow and magic broom give away her true identity. She doesn't like to give out spells very often. She prefers woodcarving – it's a much easier job.

Talking crow

Spindly fingers

Job: Woodcarver. She is also a witch – but she usually keeps that to herself!

Dislikes: Ungrateful customers

Favourite holiday spot: The Wicker Man Festival in Stornoway

Maudie

Maudie the maid is supposed to look after the triplets in the castle. However, she spends most of her time trying to avoid their pranks and stopping them from eating too many cakes. It is a very stressful job.

Maid's cap

Hot, delicious cakes

Likes: Serving the king and queen, gossiping with other servants in the castle

Dislikes: Being teased and tricked by the triplets

Goal: To stop the triplets from being naughty

When Merida returned to the castle, her mother was overjoyed to see her. However, she still insisted that Merida must marry. In desperation, Merida gave her the cake. After one bite, Elinor began to feel unwell. Merida waited for her to say she had changed her mind about a wedding, but nothing prepared her for what happened instead. Elinor turned into a huge bear! Merida knew she had to get her mother out of the castle before Fergus spotted a bear in his home and started hunting her! But before they could escape, Maudie the maid caught a glimpse of Elinor and screamed at the top of her voice.

Elinor is now so big that it is impossible for her to stay hidden inside the castle.

Hamish, Harris and Hubert

Naughty and noisy, but totally lovable, Hamish, Harris and Hubert are triple trouble. They are not scared of anything and they adore their big sister.

Merida couldn't protect her mother alone, so she turned to her little brothers for help. The wee scamps distracted their father and the clansmen with bear noises, leading them on a wild bear chase around the castle. Elinor and Merida were free to sneak away.

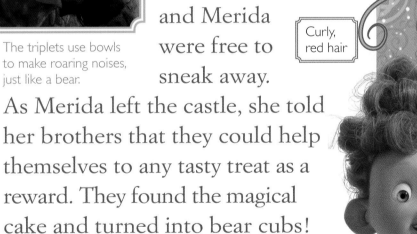

The triplets use bowls to make roaring noises, just like a bear.

Curly, red hair

As Merida left the castle, she told her brothers that they could help themselves to any tasty treat as a reward. They found the magical cake and turned into bear cubs!

Until the spell is broken, Merida will have bears for brothers!

Likes: Stealing sweets, playing pranks, getting up to mischief

Dislikes: Listening to Fergus' stories over and over again – they know every word by heart!

Least favourite food: Haggis

Elinor the bear

Elinor does not enjoy being a huge, clumsy bear. She doesn't know how to survive in the wild, but luckily, Merida can help. For the first time, Merida teaches Elinor how to behave, not the other way around.

Merida has fun showing Elinor how to catch fish in the river.

Razor-sharp claws

Glossy, black coat of fur

Merida took Elinor to find the Witch, but the old woman had disappeared, leaving only a puzzling message. It said that Merida must "mend the bond torn by pride" by the second sunrise, or her mother would stay a bear forever. While Merida tried to understand what this meant, she and Elinor began to grow closer. Mother and daughter realised that they could learn a lot from each other. Merida finally worked out how to save Elinor – they could mend their bond by mending the tapestry in the castle! Merida and Elinor returned home, but Fergus saw them. Not realising that the bear was his wife, he chased Elinor away.

After repairing the tapestry, Merida rushed to stop her father, but she was attacked by Mor'du. Elinor bravely saved

Mor'du is strong and fierce. Elinor battles him with all her strength to protect Merida.

Merida, just before the second sunrise. Merida quickly placed the tapestry over Elinor. At first nothing happened.

Merida was sure that it was all her fault. She cried to Elinor, saying how much she loved her. Suddenly, her mother returned to normal! Elinor and Merida had finally learned to listen to each other.

Merida and Elinor's love for each other changed their fate.

Mor'du

Mor'du is a bloodthirsty and cruel bear. He was once a powerful prince, but was changed into a bear by the Witch's magic. It is only after Elinor and Merida destroy him that the curse breaks and the prince's spirit is released.

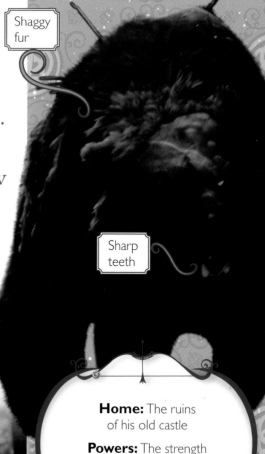

Shaggy fur

Sharp teeth

Home: The ruins of his old castle

Powers: The strength of ten men

Likes: Being stronger than anyone else, destroying his enemies at any cost

DK

LONDON, NEW YORK, MUNICH,
MELBOURNE AND DELHI

DK LONDON
Senior Editor Victoria Taylor
Senior Art Editor Lynne Moulding
Editor Lisa Stock
Editorial Assistant Lauren Nesworthy
Designer Lisa Robb
Senior Pre-Production Producer Jennifer Murray
Producer David Appleyard
Managing Editor Laura Gilbert
Managing Art Editor Maxine Pedliham
Publishing Manager Julie Ferris
Art Director Lisa Lanzarini
Publishing Director Simon Beecroft

DK DELHI
Senior Editor Garima Sharma
Editor Rahul Ganguly
Art Editor Suzena Sengupta
Assistant Art Editor Pranika Jain
Managing Editor Chitra Subramanyam
Managing Art Editor Neha Ahuja
DTP Designer Umesh Singh Rawat

Written by Beth Landis Hester
and Catherine Saunders

First published in Great Britain in 2014 by
Dorling Kindersley Limited
80 Strand, London WC2R 0RL
A Penguin Random House Company

10 9 8 7 6 5 4 3 2 1
001 – 195536 – Sep/14

A CIP catalogue record for this book is available
from the British Library.

ISBN: 978-1-40933-848-2

Colour reproduction by Alta Image Ltd, UK
Printed and bound in Slovakia by TBB, a.s.

Acknowledgements
The publisher would like to thank
Ryan Ferguson and Chelsea Alon at Disney Publishing.

Discover more at
www.dk.com